NYIRAGONGO

THE FORBIDDEN VOLCANO

Haroun Tazieff

NYIRAGONGO

THE FORBIDDEN VOLCANO

Illustrations by Pierre Bichet

Translated from the French
by J.F. Bernard

BARRON'S/WOODBURY, NEW YORK

First U.S. edition 1979 by Barron's Educational Series, Inc.

© *Flammarion, 1975*
(French language text)

All inquiries should be addressed to:
Barron's Educational Series, Inc.
113 Crossways Park Drive
Woodbury, New York 11797

Library of Congress Catalog No. 78-15023

International Standard Book No. 0-8120-5296-x

Library of Congress Cataloging in Publication Data

Tazieff, Haroun, 1914-
  Nyiragongo, the forbidden volcano.

  Translation of Niragongo.
  Bibliography: p.
  1. Nyiragongo Volcano.   I. Bichet, Pierre.
II. Title.
QE523.N9T3913   551.2'1'0967517   78-15023
ISBN 0-8120-5296-X

PRINTED IN FRANCE

CONTENTS

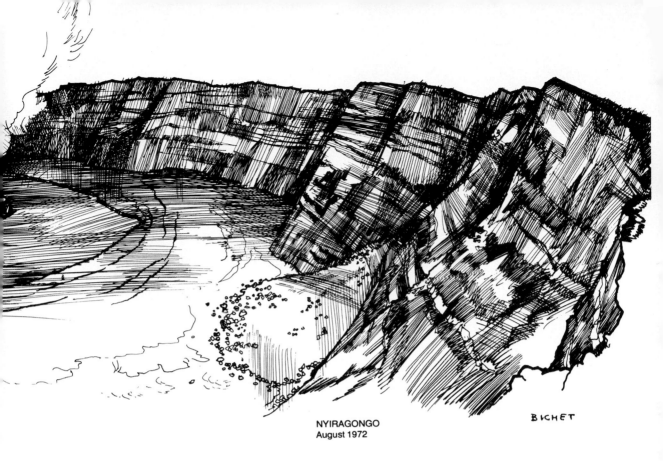

NYIRAGONGO
August 1972

BICHET

1

The forbidden volcano:
1947, 1953

Nyiragongo is an exceptional volcano, and it has played an exceptional role in my life. To begin with, it was the first volcano that I ever climbed. In September 1948, I really had no interest in volcanoes. Nyiragongo attracted me because it was a mountain, and I wanted to climb it. I had only a few hours of leisure on my hands, and it was the only peak in the area that I could ascend and descend between dawn and dusk of the same day.

My second visit took place five years later. By then, I had been bitten by the volcano bug, and I was not at all interested in climbing Nyiragongo. What I wanted was to get down into its (until then) unexplored center.

During my first visit, I had discovered a lake of molten lava at the base of Nyiragongo's great center. It was the only such lake known at that time. Thus, a passion for this volcano in particular was grafted onto my newly discovered passion for volcanoes in general. I wanted by all means to reach the shore of the lake that I had seen from the top of the volcano; the fact that it seemed a very difficult undertaking indeed only served to strengthen my determination.

The difficulties were of two kinds. The first were those created by nature herself: the vertical drop and the obvious fragile state of the inner wall of the volcano, the abundance of sulphurous fumes, the infernal heat. The second kind were those created by human beings. Granted that governments by their very nature are not inclined to favor individual undertakings of any kind, I must say that the governments with which I had to deal were not only unfavorably disposed, but hostile in the extreme. And that is why, for me, Nyiragongo remained for years "the forbidden volcano."

First explorations

The volcanic nature of the Virunga (Bufumbira) Mountains was first recognized, in 1891, by Franz Stuhlman. They had been discovered and named in 1861, by John Hanning Speke. On March 14, 1876, Sir Henry Morton Stanley saw "the three cones of Virunga in the west-northwest." Stuhlman described this chain as he saw it from the other side—that is, from the bank of Lake Edward—as follows: "About ten o'clock, I was awakened by the man on watch, who burst into my tent shouting, 'Sir, the sky is on fire!' A joyous thought crossed my mind: It was the volcano! I ran out of the tent and almost shouted for joy when I saw that the brightness of the sky was not due to a brush fire. It was too bright for that; the source of that light was much more powerful than any mere surface fire. The sight of it was proof enough that the chain of the Virungas was still active. Our guides assured us that there were times, at night, when this mountain, Kirunga Visoke (which, according to them, was four to six days' march from where we were), shot fire into the air and made noises that sounded like the lowing of cows and rifle shots. They interpreted these noises as manifestations of an evil spirit."

Three years later, other German explorers, Count Adolf von Götzen and W. von Prittwitz, were the first Europeans not only to reach this chain of mountains but also to climb one of the most active of its volcanoes: Nyiragongo.

Their expedition, after a five-month trek from the coast of the Indian Ocean, pitched camp near Lake Mohassi, in Rwanda, the evening of May 27, 1894. The sky in the northwest was bright in the surrounding darkness. "With this spectacular evidence," von Götzen wrote, "I could no longer doubt that the Virunga Mountains were indeed active volcanoes. The most westerly of these cones, named Kirunga Tshagongo, seemed to be in full eruption."

Von Götzen named this volcanic range "Virunga" (the plural form of *Kirunga*), and that is the name by which it is known today. The name of Bufumbira is used only in the western part of the mountains.

It took the explorers ten days to travel the fifty-five or so miles to the range. Every night, the volcano treated them to a display of lights that attracted them as a flame attracts moths. Von Götzen's account is quite interesting, not only because it describes the very first ascent of one of the Virunga peaks, but also because it evidences the difficulties of climbing a mountain in central Africa at that time:

The volcano shines in the night like a column of fire. On Thursday, June 7, 1894, after having walked for six hours in a northerly direction, we reached its foot. Prittwitz and I were accompanied by eighteen strapping bearers (two men for each load), by a corporal who had once climbed Rounsoro with Franz Stuhlman, and by two soldiers. Our guides were two diminutive Batoua tribesmen, supplied by the local chief, armed with bows and arrows.

We first crossed several hills of volcanic origin and finally came to a lava field three or four miles across. Here, the terrain began to be marked by crevasses. The many bizarre cracks, ridges, and mounds, resulting from the cooling of streams of lava, did not make it ideal for walking. We followed a trail made by elephant hunters which led, after many windings and turnings, to the foot of the mountain.

We began the slow climb at half past two. Earlier, we had sent our mules back to the rear with the Somali because it was too difficult for them to get across the cracks in the lava. We soon reached clumps of brush which, as we went on, gradually took on the appearance of a dense virgin forest. We were soon in almost complete darkness. Then, quite suddenly, the trail ended. At that moment, our guides, taking advantage of our lack of surveillance, disappeared into the thick vegetation.

From then on, every step we took meant hard work with our axes and machetes. I soon realized that it would be dark before we could reach the depression that separated the cone from a secondary crater located much further down toward the south. We were therefore obliged to spend the night in the midst of this impenetrable jungle—after clearing an area large enough to be able to pitch our tents.

The following day, we left our tents and our porters behind

Double page following: The eastern volcanoes of the Virunga Mountains.

and struck out with our three Askaris. Our hunting knives were very useful to us, but were nonetheless much less effective than the sabers of our soldiers. It was a real pleasure to watch the branches and vines falling all around us as the soldiers worked. Even so, we moved slowly because all the cutting and hacking often caused more vines and branches to fall and obstruct our way. Fortunately, the ascent was not very steep, and we were confident that we could continue moving directly toward that recessed ledge which was our first objective.

It took the five of us nine hours of work to cut a path about a mile and a half long.

Toward noon, we returned to our tents for a rest. From there, we dispatched a man to Kersting with a letter describing our predicament and telling him that we would no doubt be gone longer than we had planned. We also asked him to send out a party with water, food, and goats.

We worked hard the next day and added another mile and a half to the trail. The vegetation was now even denser and more contorted than before. Often, enormous tree trunks were lying across our path and required detours that were increasingly difficult to cut as the climb became more steep. Even though we rested thirty minutes after every thirty minutes of work, our strength was obviously ebbing. Unless we found clearer ground soon, we would have to send back for more men, and that would mean another day's delay. We had no choice, meanwhile, but to continue moving forward. Once the main branches were cut off of small trees, we would push and pull on the trees with all our might to try to disengage them from the tangle of interlacing branches and thus clear a way for ourselves. Often, a milky sap would come out of a tree whose acidity was dangerous to our eyes. And, of course, there were thorns everywhere; consequently, scratches and punctures everywhere.

At two o'clock, our supply party arrived. Kersting had sent us two new guides familiar with the jungle. Even though they bore a marked resemblance to our first two Batoua guides, they claimed to belong to an entirely different tribe. Be that as it may, as soon as our eyes were off them for a moment, they disappeared among the trees in the same manner as their predecessors.

Thus, without guides, we nonetheless set out at seven o'clock.

Our party now consisted of twelve men. The ground was even more irregular than before and walking was more difficult, for the soft layer of humus was patchy and the pure lava was exposed in many areas. Finally, at 9:30, we reached the plateau between the peaks. We were at the foot of the larger of the two, the slope of which was quite steep and entirely without vegetation. The summit was wrapped in thick clouds.

We rested for a few minutes, then began the ascent, following a straight line on the southern flank of the volcano, over terrain studded with sharp rocks. Our climb seemed to become more arduous by the minute and we found ourselves clambering over walls and blocks of lava while heaps of trachyte on the ground cut our feet and made walking hazardous. My body servant, who was barefoot, was forced to remain behind. By then, we were gasping for breath and our pulses were racing. I had to stop every twenty minutes for a rest period.

Marbrouk, one of our bearers, was ahead of me, scrambling over the rocks. Suddenly, I saw him stop and raise his arms, as though trying to signal me, but a violent clap, like thunder, obliterated the sound of his voice. I gathered what little strength I had left and caught up with him. What I saw took my breath away.

At my feet yawned a crater the size of ten Coliseums. We were standing on its rim, and its wall was a straight drop down. At first glance, the entire crater was obscured by clouds of vapor, but then a gust of wind swept away these clouds and we could see the opposite side of the crater's interior. Toward the north, we made out the openings of two pits as regular in shape as though they were man-made. Clouds of vapor were rising continuously from one of these, and, at irregular but frequent intervals, there was a deep rumble that was half thunder and half whistle. Whenever it was heard, it made my men draw back in astonishment and fear.

Having no point of reference to serve in determining the diameter of the crater, we decided to try to walk around it. I gave our people permission to return to camp without us because it would have been very uncomfortable for them to wait for us in the cold, damp wind, crouched on these sharp rocks. Moreover, most of them already had cuts on their feet; several were too susceptible to vertigo to follow us around the narrow rim of the

crater. We therefore departed alone on this dangerous phase of our undertaking. To our left was the crater with its sheer interior wall; to our right, the exterior slopes, also steep, which seemed to us like a bottomless abyss because of the thick clouds that constantly obscured them.

After two hours' walk—possible only because of our cleated mountain climbing boots—we were back at our point of departure. We could then have returned to camp. There remained a question to be answered: What was the cause of the reddish glow that we saw every night in the sky? At my insistence, we undertook another trek around the crater, but this time several hundred yards further down the slope. It transpired that I had underestimated the distance involved and overestimated the strength that we had left. It became obvious when darkness overtook us that we would not be able to return to camp that day. And, as a sharp wind arose, we began to plan how we would spend the night. First, we leveled a stretch of ground under a thicket and, with branches, fashioned a lean-to that would serve to protect us from the wind, for it was begining to get quite cold and it had begun to drizzle. We had only our daytime clothing and no coverings of any kind. We did not even have a drop of liquor to warm ourselves. We attempted to make a fire and finally succeeded, using strips of cloth torn from our clothing and blowing until we were dizzy in an effort to ignite the green kindling that we had collected. We sat there, shivering, our teeth chattering, chilled to the bone by the dampness. It seemed to me that the wind was as cold as the depths of winter in Silesia.

The marriage of fire and water

The many visitors who climb Nyiragongo today can hardly imagine the difficulties that Count von Götzen and his companions had to overcome. It is always so: the first time that something is done, the problems are incredibly more complex than on subsequent occasions. And this holds true not only for mountain climbing.

Today, the plateau located between the principal peak and the Shaheru

Shaheru crater seen from the upper slopes of Nyiragongo. Note the black volcanic rocks in the foreground and, further down, the vegetation.

Baruta crater, flanking Nyiragongo.

(its impressive satellite to the south), is accessible in three hours' time to
an ordinary climber following a trail through the jungle. Another trail leads
through Baruta, the northern satellite, to the same shelf. From there, it is
only another hour's climb to the summit. The total time required today is
no more than four hours to reach a point that an explorer required four days
of struggle to reach.

Muhavura, the easternmost volcano in the Virunga Mountains.

Beyond the plantations are Mikeno (13,618 feet) and Karisimbi (14,850 feet).

The Virunga Mountains, which consist entirely of geologically young volcanoes, stretch from east to west for about fifty-five miles. They lie within a gigantic ditch—or rift, as geologists call it—that zigzags across eastern Africa from Ethiopia to Mozambique. The rift is a deep valley marking a point at which portions (or plates) of the earth's crust are separating. In the rift, the volcanoes develop at points where the magma under the earth's crust wells up. The magma is the layer of viscous matter that lies between the earth's core and its crust, as the white of an egg is between the yolk and the shell. Under pressure the earth's thin crust cracks, and molten magma of the mantle wells up to reach the surface of the earth. That, in its simplest terms, is what volcanism is.

In practice, volcanoes are more likely to appear in areas where rifts, running in different directions, intersect. This is because the cracks that develop through which the magma rises to the surface are largest and most likely to become permanent at these points. Thus it is that the Virunga Mountains developed at the point at which the western branch of the East African Rift system intersects the north-south rifts. There are eight important mountains in this chain, the highest of which has an altitude of almost 15,000 feet and the lowest an altitude of almost 10,000 feet. In addition to these, there are a dozen more modest peaks certain of which—like Shaheru and Baruta, which flank Nyiragongo on either side—would be impressive volcanoes in their own right if they were not dwarfed by their mighty neighbors.

Successive eruptions over the past one or two billion years have resulted in a buildup of billions of cubic yards of lava; that immense volume of lava comprises the Virunga Mountains. This range of mountains eventually blocked completely the immense valley through which the ancestor of the Nile River had flowed. Since then, the water has accumulated upstream of this natural dam, inundating the valleys in a body of water now known as Lake Kivu. This lake is especially picturesque because the mountain peaks cut the lake into narrow blue gulfs bounded by densely wooded crests, vermillion jungles, and the sparkling green of cultivated plantations. When its waters reached high enough, they escaped through an overflow to form the torrential Rusizi. In this way, waters which once flowed into the Mediterranean now reach instead the Atlantic Ocean, via Lake Tanganyika, the Lufira, and the Congo.

The southern slopes of Nyiragongo and its neighbor, Nyamuragira, go down several hundred yards beneath the surface of Lake Kivu. Thus it often happens that streams of molten lava from these two volcanoes flow down into the lake. That is precisely what happened during the first eruption I saw at this point. This phenomenon serves to increase the height and the width of this natural dam. In May 1948, Nyamuragira was split open by a fissure running for several miles on its southern flank. Molten rock, at the rate of thousands of tons per minute, flowed from the two extremities of the fissure. It took several days of continuous flow for the lava to reach the lake. When it did, I witnessed one of those phenomenon that often gives volcanoes their paradoxical aspect: the peaceful comingling of fire and water.

I, like everyone else, expected that the contact of the lava flow with the waters of the lake would result in an extraordinarily impressive, and possibly dangerous, pyrotechnical display. For that reason, we were prepared to observe this display from a rowboat at a very respectable distance from the point of contact. As it happened, our caution was unnecessary. The molten rock reached the lake and slid into the water with wholly unexpected serenity and, indeed, in virtual silence. As the sinuous line of thick red fluid met the water, a rising cloud of vapor was the only indication that anything unusual was taking place.

Still exercising much caution, we moved closer. Another paradox: the water was not boiling. In fact, it was not even hot to the touch. In spots, it was tepid, but mostly it seemed to be at normal temperature.

If we had taken time to think about it beforehand, we would not have been surprised. It takes a great deal of energy to bring water to the boiling point. (Compare, for instance, the time that it takes, over the same fire, to bring water, oil, and metal to a temperature of 212°F.) Water has a capacity for absorbing heat without a rapid rise in its own temperature. What happened here was that the water absorbed the heat of the lava with virtually no perceptible rise in temperature. It also helped, of course, that only the outer layer of lava came into contact with the water because it immediately formed a shell of solidified lava. This shell, in combination with the gaseous bubbles within it, effectively served to insulate the still-molten rock inside the shell from the surrounding water. Also, it must be remembered that only an extremely small proportion of the water in the lake came into direct contact with the lava and reached the boiling point. This small amount of water, lightened by dilatation*, immediately rose from the lake as a cloud of vapor and, almost immediately, cooled. In this way, the momentary rise in the water's temperature, caused by contact with the lava flow, was dissipated throughout the lake. And the overall rise in temperature was so slight as to be virtually imperceptible. It goes without saying, of course, that at the very spot where the lava came into contact with the lake, the water boiled violently. It was the end of any fish who happened to be in that particular spot at that given moment. In fact, we pulled aboard several fishes that we saw floating alongside our rowboat, and it was obvious that they were at least parboiled, if not thoroughly cooked.

This rapid dissipation of heat in a large volume of cold water also explains why we saw a cloud of steam only where the lava actually touched the lake. Elsewhere, the bubbles from the boiling water were created under several inches (or, further out from the shore, several feet) of water, and they did not reach the surface to form steam because, in rising through the cold water, they contracted and, in a very short time, became liquid again.

All these technical considerations did not detract from our fascination

---

*The density of any material—gas, liquid, or solid—decreases as its temperature rises.

Mikeno, as seen from Nyiragongo.

with the spectacle before us. We watched as though hypnotized as the flow of lava spread beneath the surface of the lake. As we drifted in six to ten feet of water, we could see the molten interior of the lava glowing through the already solidified exterior shell.

A view of Nyiragongo from beyond the jungle to the north.

Later I was to witness the same phenomenon during the underwater eruptions of the Capelinhos Volcano in the Azores and of the Surtsey and Eldfell in Iceland. I was then determined to revise the hypothesis that explains how those colossal accumulations of volcanic tuffs (which are called palagonites) result from the breakup of underwater lava flows. It had been thought that these were explosions caused by the actual contact between the lava (at 2,300°F) and the water, or by a contraction of the lava crust owing to its sudden contact with the water. I tried to demonstrate that this was not the case at all, and that these layers of volcanic ash, which are sometimes hundreds of yards in thickness and spread out over enormous areas, were the result of innumerable explosions. The explosions were caused by overheated vapor that had become trapped under the flows of molten lava erupting from underwater craters. These flows are then thrown up into the sea by the explosion of these eruptive gases.

It has already been six years since I published my first article on this subject. Other articles followed, adducing new proofs. Nonetheless, many geologists still accept the traditional explanations for this phenomenon—explanations that they no doubt accepted in the first place without discussion. It is not easy to give up an idea once one has accepted it as the truth.

In the eighty years since the discovery of Nyamuragira, the volcano has erupted about ten times. On three such occasions, the lava from the mountain reached the waters of Lake Kivu: in 1912, from the Karisimbi crater; in 1938, from the Tahambene crater; and in 1948, from the Muhuboli crater. All these craters are on the southern flank of the volcano.

In the brief span since von Götzen's discovery, however, Nyiragongo has not had a single eruption outside its walls. Nonetheless, its activity in the lake of molten lava at the bottom of the pit is both extraodinary and spectacular. It is quite rare that such an increase in heat can be maintained for more than a few weeks or months especially since heat is constantly being lost through contact with the air. During our successive expeditions, we calculated the expenditure of energy involved, and, although using different methods, we always arrived at the following figures: 75 to 150 KW per square yard per second.

A visit to Nyiragongo

Certainly, I did not think of all those things during my first visit to Nyiragongo. In fact, I did not think much about volcanoes in general, except (like most of my fellow geologists) to think of them as a phenomenon without much importance compared to such things as sedimentation, continental drift, or glaciation. Although I was an ardent mountain climber, I had been separated from my beloved Alps by the war. I was still impervious to the attractions of volcanism because of my training in a kind of geological science that was more conformist and self-satisfying than it was alive and pulsating with new ideas. I was willing, however, to indulge myself in my avocation by climbing the slopes of a volcano. My impression of it was that of a thick jungle without beauty to which long strands of moss, hanging from the branches of sandalwood trees, gave an eerily subaqueous aspect. The gigantic heatherlike vegetation of the slopes sometimes reaches a height of thirty to forty-five feet, and in equatorial regions grows to an altitude of about three miles. It overwhelmed the green of the other vegetation by the near-black of its tiny foliage. But the jungle ended with this vegetation. Beyond that point, there was only tree-sized ragwort looking like immense salads and beautiful giant lobelia with their high stalks covered by hundreds of small flowers descending in tight, regular spirals.

It was the dry season, and a fine cloud of dust of many months' duration hung in the air, reducing visibility and tinging everything with gray. The dust reduced the shapes of distant objects to fuzzy outlines. All these things added little to my enjoyment. Nyiragongo, I kept reminding myself, was a mountain. But I confess that, as a lover of the Alps, I found little consolation in that fact. Without too much difficulty, I reached the summit. There was a narrow circular ridge or rim, separating the top of the ex-

The narrow rim of Nyiragongo's caldera.

terior slope from the sheer drop to the interior of the volcano. The view down was impressive, and it made up somewhat for the lack of visibility and for the ease of the ascent. (I had not yet read von Götzen's account of his ascent, and I had blithely made use of the path up the mountain cleared and maintained by the rangers in Virunga National Park.)

In appearance, the crater was actually a cylindrical caldera—a crater whose sides had given way and collapsed. The caldera was about 5,000 feet in diameter. I could make out the bottom through the clouds of steam emitted from a large central pit. From time to time, I caught glimpses of the edges of the pit itself on the floor of the caldera. None of this seemed terribly interesting to me. What did hold my attention was the interior wall of the caldera which dropped abruptly from the rim to the floor. It appealed to my mountain climber's instincts. It was a straight drop of perhaps 600 feet and, as such, offered an opportunity for a challenging desent. It occurred to me that this perhaps was what made it worthwhile to climb Nyiragongo after all.

I was lying flat on my stomach, leaning on my elbows overlooking the

Nyiragongo's caldera viewed from an airplane.

Opposite: Nyiragongo's outside wall is covered by countless streams of solidified lava which, along with layers of lapilli and ash, make up the volcano's cone.

immense hole. I remained there for almost an hour hoping that the steam would clear enough for me to see the whole thing more clearly. To make the time pass, I kept busy examining what I could see of the interior wall for footholds. In time, I evolved at least a half-dozen plans of descent.

It was already dark by the time I emerged from the jungle on the slopes, and then only after I had run almost without stopping from the summit. I swore to myself that this first visit to a volcanic mountain would also be my last. It was to be only six months later that I turned myself into a per-jurer at Nyamuragira during an eruption. That was the first step in a scientific adventure that has continued now for more than a quarter of a century.

To observe that eruption, I had pitched my camp near the Kituro crater, at the uphill end of the fissure which, for the past several months, had been spouting gas and lava. From that spot, I spent a good deal of time watching the flattened summit of neighboring Nyiragongo which was only about 1,500 yards away. The reddish glow of its smokey crest, especially on cloudless nights, drew my eyes like a magnet. It brought to mind the fiery pit at the bottom of that vast caldera of which I still had a vivid recollection. What was that fire, I wondered. What was its nature? What was the form and the meaning of the mighty furnace that, according to the unanimous testimony of the older people living in the area, dated back twenty years? I was aware that it was nothing more than molten lava, but human curiosity—to say nothing of geological curiosity—required a more comprehensive explanation. I learned from several planters in the area, and from the old chief of the Banyarwanda aborigenes, that this same kind of curiosity had inspired several rather daring individuals over the years to try climbing down into the caldera in order to reach the great central pit which was the source of the smoke rising from the volcano. No one, however, had yet succeeded in this undertaking.

I often thought of the descent, and I was always surprised that no experienced alpinist had ever been tempted to undertake the descent to the foot of the interior wall. I had already noticed several ways in which it could be done. I could only suppose that amateurs, even the most audacious amateurs, had not been accustomed to cliffs and were discouraged by the nearly vertical drop and virgin appearance of that circular wall. For an experienced climber, on the other hand, such considerations would only be an added inducement. I turned the project over in my mind from various aspects, but I could do nothing about it. I had been given permission by my chief, at the Congolese Geological Service, to observe the eruption of the Kituro crater. As long as that eruption lasted, I felt obliged to remain at my post. As it turned out, Kituro was in eruption for five months.

The descent into the caldera of Nyiragongo can be described as a "descent into hell—it is no mere figure of speech. As the weeks passed, I often spoke to the people in the surrounding area about the volcano. To them, the volcano was the resting place of souls after death. It was not seen as a place of heavenly delight, nor was it a pit of infernal suffering, expiatory or not. It was simply the "underworld" as the ancients thought of it; that is, a place where the souls of one's ancestors found a lasting home among the flames. These stories and explanations were made either in Kiswahili—a language imported from the eastern coast of Africa (which I spoke fluently at the time) or in Kinyarwanda, which was the local language. In the latter case, I had the help and guidance of my friend Alyette de Munck, who had lived in the area since her childhood.

I had met Alyette and her husband Adrien at the very beginning of my involvement with volcanic eruptions. Inexperienced as I was, I had come very close to letting my two assistants and myself be surrounded by fast-moving lava flows. As soon as we saw our situation, we made a dash toward safety—if I may describe as a "dash" the progress of three men, each carrying about 125 pounds of equipment. Eventually, soaked by the rain and sweating from every pore, we stumbled into a huge flower-filled garden along the shore of one of Lake Kivu's bays. In the middle of the garden was a peaceful, rambling, single-storied house half-hidden among the bougainvillea and the hibiscus plants. Two blond children were playing noisily on a huge veranda, and smiling servants moved busily about their chores. We stood and gaped unabashedly at what, to us, seemed a heavenly vision. For days, we had been subjected to burning ash, lava flows, impassable thickets, daggerlike thorns, razor-edged rocks, chilling rain, and even hunger. Our muscles were trembling with exhaustion, and our hands, arms, and knees were covered with bruises and cuts. Then, suddenly, we found ourselves in a garden like something out of a nineteenth-century novel.

As we stood there, I saw a European man wearing khaki shorts walking toward us. He was smiling broadly, welcoming us to this paradise, but, strangely, he did not seem at all surprised to find us there.

An hour later, having bathed and changed into dry clothing, I was at the table enjoying a British-style lunch and putting out of my mind all the discomforts and troubles of the past two days. While I ate, Adrien explained why he had not been surprised at the bizarre apparition on his lawn. His wife had known for several hours before our arrival that there were three refugees (which is what we were) moving in a southeasterly direction ahead of a lava flow. There was only one place in which we could emerge from the jungle, and that was at Adrien's and Alyette's home. In fact, at dawn, the villagers had spotted us, wobbling under our loads of supplies and making headway with much difficulty, to the west of the Buheno property.

For the next six months, Buheno was the point of departure for all my volcanic forays. For the next twenty-five years, it served a similar function for all my expeditions to Nyiragongo. In fact, Alyette and Adrien accompanied me on those expeditions, beginning as soon as the day after my rather sudden appearance at their home. They were both accomplished

woodspeople. Adrien was a prospector who had spent twenty-five of his forty years searching for gold and tin throughout the Congo, Burundi, and Rwanda, only to end up finding a superb bed of tungsten. Alyette, for her part, was only about thirty years old at the time and had spent almost her whole life in the Kivu area. She had a thorough familiarity with the region because she had traveled across it in the only way that it is possible to learn an area; that is, on foot. She seemed absolutely indefatigable. When she did suffer from the duration or difficulty of a trek, she never uttered a word of complaint but did her very best to cover it up. Her courage, unfortunately, was often to be tried by future events. Adrien died suddenly in 1966. One year later, her two sons, aged 21 and 23, were brutally murdered in the Congo in the most atrocious circumstances.

Adrien and Alyette were my cherished companions during the five months of Kituro's eruption. My other companion, Paya, who was a kind of general assistant and factotum, was a good man, and a courageous one. We had worked together for three years, and I had the utmost confidence in him. There were three occasions during those years when we faced death together, and Paya had been absolutely unwavering in his determination to stick with me to the end. Still, Paya was too lacking in initiative and decisiveness for me to take certain risks while he and I were alone. Now, the moral and material support of my new friends made such risks acceptable.

A high-altitude tropical forest.

At the edge of the pit

It was not until August of 1948 that I was finally able to return to Nyira-gongo. The volcano's reputation for inaccessibility was so well established that even I was impressed. And I am not that easily impressed about that sort of thing. Every time I spoke to anyone about my idea of going down into the volcano, I was greeted with pessimism—except, of course, in the case of Alyette and Adrien de Munck. However, I was not counting on Alyette and Adrien to accompany me. Adrien's health was already too precarious for that, and Alyette had never done any mountain climbing. In fact, I had considerable difficulty in finding an experienced companion. Those who were both experienced enough and young enough for such an undertaking were very rare in this area. Finally, I happened upon Georges Tondeur, who allowed me to convince him of the feasibility of the project. Georges, while not a mountain man, had had some experience in the Alps and he knew how to handle a safety rope. Moreover, he was willing to risk the descent—which was an essential point.

Before we could start down the caldera wall, however, we had first to convince the Banyarwanda bearers, who had accompanied us up Nyira-gongo, to let us go down. The caldera, they argued, was the kingdom of the spirits, the place where souls went after death. If we went down while we were alive, we would never return because the spirits would not allow it. I still do not know how much of their opposition was based on fear for our safety and how much on fear of angering the spirits. In any case, our stubbornness finally proved to be greater than theirs. Their desolate, re-signed expressions as they watched us rope up and climb down the first few steps, was that of adults who stand helpless before the dangerous antics of spoiled and uncontrollable children.

We had just come level with the first projection in the wall, which re-quired caution, when we heard a shout from above. We looked up and saw four round heads peering over the rim, outlined against the sky like disem-bodied skulls. There was something funny about the sight, and it put me in a good mood. One of the four heads shouted: "*Kama weye unafika chini, chini kabisa, na kama unasiya baba yango, useme ye ninapenda ye ngufu, na ninakukumbuka ye aiku zote, na heshimu ye.*" ("If you get to the bot-tom, the very bottom, and you see my father, tell him that I love him very much, that I still think of him, and that I honor him.") We were now con-stituted messengers to the nether world.

There were footholds and handholds in abundance along the wall. The problem was not to find a place on which to rest a hand or foot, but to choose supports that would not give way under our weight or under traction. An active volcano is constantly shaken by microscopic quakes and quite often by more or less violent shocks that cause the rocks in its walls to loosen. These rocks eventually become loose and if you take hold of even a large one and give it a tug in the wrong direction, it is likely to come off in your hand. This situation made it necessary for me to use extreme caution, and we were careful to pick our rocks one at a time, observing all the rules of safety that we had been taught both by technique and by experience. We hesitated several times over the route to take, and two or three slightly protruding ledges required extra care. Thus, it took us two whole hours to reach the huge horizontal landing that was our goal. Once there, however, we indulged in one of those explosions of joy familiar to alpinists who attain a peak—except that our peak was, in fact, a floor and a bottom rather than a summit. It was not even the bottom of the bottom but that did not matter to us.

No ghost and no demon came to interfere with our celebration. It occurred to us that they may have been residing lower down. Then we set out, running, for the edge of the pit. Except for a few crevices, which we took in a single leap, the terrace (which was about 200 feet in diameter), presented no obstacle to us. It is true that, although we ran only a few seconds, we were breathless by the time we reached the edge; but running at an altitude of 13,500 feet tends to have that effect.

At the bottom of the pit was the most unexpected, extraordinary spectacle that I have ever seen: an enormous lake (at least, it seemed enormous to me) of boiling lava covering about one-third of the large circle forming the floor of the caldera. The heat radiated by the lava singed our faces, even though we were about 600 feet above it. Huge waves of lava stirred the gray surface of the lake and enabled us to glimpse, briefly, the gold color of the molten rock beneath. Actually, they were not waves, although ripples emanated from them; rather, they were bubbles of from fifteen to fifty feet in diameter rising to the surface and revealing, momentarily, the interior depths.

This was the source of the nocturnal reddish glow which, for the past twenty-five years, had haloed Nyiragongo and which, on certain nights, was visible at a distance of sixty or seventy miles. This lake, a permanent cauldron of molten lava, was the only such lake in the world known at that time. The exaltation we felt at the sight of this splendid spectacle almost overwhelmed the excitement of discovering it, of having succeeded in an undertaking that everyone regarded as doomed to failure, and of anticipating future investigations of this phenomenon.

It is my nature to want always to go forward. For that reason, no doubt, even while my eyes were drinking in the sight before me, my mind was al-

The interior wall of the caldera, illuminated by the molten lava.

ready racing ahead to forthcoming research projects, problems of material, supplies and personnel, technical questions, speculation on the importance of our discovery, and a thousand other things the whole of which had to do with the existence of this lake and the volcano observatory on which construction, no doubt, would begin almost immediately. One such observatory had been built in 1912, on Kilauea volcano, near the lip of its celeberated pit known as Halemaumau ("Home of the Eternal Fire"). The lava lake of Halemaumau had been discovered in 1823, but had disappeared during the violent eruption of 1924. In the twelve-year existence of the observatory, the study of volcanism had made more progress than it had during the preceding hundred years.

The presence of this new lake meant that the essential elements of volcanic eruption—that is, gas and molten rock—would once more be constantly available and accessible to observers. It would be possible to measure them and study them almost at leisure, to record variations in the magnetic field, to measure tremors in the earth, the swellings or deflations of the earth's surface while at the same time observing what was happening within the caldera itself. These things are all practically the *sine qua non* of volcanology. The lack of such opportunity is one of the reasons why geologists, when they do not have access to permanent volcanic activity, make such slow progress in the knowledge of this complex and capricious phenomenon. It follows, therefore, that when an active volcano is discovered—which happens very rarely indeed—full advantage must be taken of the situation. The fact was that, of the ten such volcanoes known at that time (an eleventh has since been discovered in Ethiopia), not a single one of them was equipped with an observatory. The only observatories were on volcanoes that had shown a prolonged period of activity: Kilauea and Vesuvius. But even these stations had lost much of their usefulness because the volcanoes on which they were located had become quiescent or dormant, Kilauea in 1924 and Vesuvius twenty years later. Since then, like the fifteen other observatories then in existence—Japanese, for the most part—they struggled along, waiting for their sleeping volcanoes to stir.

What we had just discovered on Nyiragongo was the kind of activity most favorable to in-depth study: a lake of molten lava. I say "the most favorable" because a lake of this kind is the least violent, the most approachable, and the most fruitful for researchers of the various kinds of volcanic activity. Since it was the only one of its kind known at that time, I had not the slightest doubt that it would immediately become the site of an observatory fully equipped with the most modern instruments, manned by a staff of researchers, subsidized with all necessary funds, and so forth. It seemed logical to assume that the research program that had come to a halt with the disappearance of the Kilauea lake, twenty-five years earlier, would be taken up again; and that, given the formidable technical advances that had been made in that quarter-century, the new observatory would race ahead in the exploration of volcanic secrets. All these things occupied my thoughts as my mind raced ahead, while my eyes remained fixed on the extraordinary sight at the bottom of the pit.

My euphoria lasted for a relatively long time. It went on for months, despite the lack of any interest on the part of my superior in the Geological Service, despite the indifference of the regional scientific community, and despite the obstacles, veiled in amiability, erected by those whose job it was to defend the Virunga volcanoes—that is, the authorities in the Bureau of National Parks. The word *defend*, in this context, should have meant "protect." Instead, it came to mean "put off-limits."

The mortal sin that I had committed was that of expressing independent opinions from the very beginning of the volcanological mission that I was supposed to undertake within their bailiwick. I had then aggravated the situation by succeeding in an undertaking that they had regarded as impossible and, moreover, doing it without their knowledge or cooperation. For the next ten years, I was *persona non grata* to the gentlemen of the National Parks, which meant that I was not allowed to remain in Virunga National Park, or to undertake any kind of systematic study of Nyiragongo, or, of course, to establish an observatory. It was a hard lesson. In those ten years, an observatory would have made it possible for the science of volcanology, which was at a very modest stage of development, to make a great leap forward. And, so far as I was concerned, it would have spared me the enormous effort that I had to expend to revive that science in western Europe where, since World War II, it had practically disappeared.

Not only was the observatory project relegated to the waste basket by the so-called competent authorities, but I eventually found myself out of a job. My administrative superiors, intimidated by the omnipotence of the head of the National Parks Bureau, had suggested that I give up such childish things as volcanology and get down to serious work; that is, to "real geology." I therefore resigned from the Geological Service. Still haunted by the wish to work in volcanology, and by the desire to prove wrong those who denied the importance of that study, I felt very much alone and very helpless. Most geologists at that time were indifferent to volcanic phenomena; most geophysicists held volcanology in contempt. The great European volcanologists of the pre-war period had virtually disappeared. Either they were too old to be active, or they had lost their following and their papers went unread. Volcanology at that period was going around in circles, occupying itself with academic discussions on data accumulated twelve to fifteen years before. It was a discouraging situation.

It was pride, perhaps more than a love of science, that kept me going in the years that followed; for it would be a decade before things began to change. "Forget it," people would tell me, "you can't fight the establishment." But I was determined; and being told that I could not win only served to strengthen my determination. During that long struggle, I was not entirely alone. I had the discreet, calm, and effective support of a friend: Professor Ivan de Magnée. He had been one of my teachers when I was a student, and I had studied geophysics and the principles of mining under him. After I graduated, Professor de Magnée had offered me a job as his assistant in his Bruxelles laboratory. It was he who, after the war, encouraged me to put aside my dreams of Central Asia—the mountain climber's heaven, if there is one—and go to Africa instead. After my volcanological mutiny, he was the only geologist of stature and reputation to support me in what, between 1948 and 1958, appeared to be a solitary, and sometimes infantile, battle on behalf of a hopeless cause. Without Professor de Magnée, I would perhaps have begun to doubt, not only myself, but also the value and validity of my scientific goals. Whenever I did have such doubts in those long years, I always drew strength and comfort from his counsel.

The secret team

Since I was banished from the national park in which Nyiragongo was located, there was little I could do even to visit the volcano. I was without private means, and travel—to say nothing of expeditions—costs a great deal of money. It was five years before I could return to that extraordinary volcano, the recollection of which strengthened in me the determination to explore it thoroughly from top to bottom. I financed the visit by a speaking tour in the Congo. Such tours are pleasant enough under certain aspects, and less pleasant under others.

In 1953, my second visit to Nyiragongo was, from a personal standpoint, certainly worthwhile, even though I could not go down farther than we had five years earlier and even though I could not undertake any real research because of lack of money. First of all, I had the somewhat perverse pleasure of defying the authorities by returning to the volcano. But, even more, it pleased me no end once again to be able to leave the beaten path and strike out on my own, at least in a figurative sense. I should add that, in a literal sense, there was then only one path leading to the summit of Nyiragongo—a path which had been frayed by elephants and then enlarged somewhat by machetes. (Today there is a second path, on the north slope.) We could not use that path, however, because it was guarded by rangers. We resolved the problem by doing a bit of reconnoitering in Adrien's little single-engine plane and discovering another elephant trail. This new access enabled us to evade detection and, without too much difficulty, make our way through the thick jungle that covers the foot of the mountain. As an added precaution, we undertook the climb in the middle of the night. The preceding afternoon, I had driven across the frontier into Uganda in my jeep, just as though I were leaving the Congo for good. And then, having duped the guards, I drove back after nightfall and joined my friends who, with a group of bearers, were waiting at the foot of the elephant trail that we had sighted from the air.

The ascent came off without incident. The next day, however, the weather took a turn for the worse, alternating between drizzle and fog. We could see neither the slopes nor the surrounding peaks. Nyiragongo's caldera itself was full of steam and visibility was practically nil. Nonetheless, we began our descent. We were a fairly large party because a half-dozen friends of Adrien's and Alyette's had joined us. Two of them, Louis Tormoz and Jean Deru, were good climbers. Tormoz, in fact, had been a professional mountain guide for many years, but the others were all beginners. When we were halfway down, I decided to put Tormoz in charge of the rest of the climb so that I could finish the descent by myself and get to the edge of the pit. The fact that we were moving so slowly, and especially the fear that the bad weather might force us to give the whole thing up, made me decide to do this. As it turned out, I had just reached the edge of the pit when the fog became so thick that the rest of the party was brought to a halt. I spent a rather uncomfortable night on the hard terrace of the caldera, but my discomfort was nothing compared to that of the others. The five of them spent the entire night hanging motionless against the wall of the caldera. They still have a vivid recollection of it, in which cold, humidity, and numb arms and legs feature prominently.

During that interminable night, I tried several times to get a bit of sleep, and a bit of heat, by stretching out across one of the fissures giving off steam. Every time that I did so, I was awakened in a few minutes by a trickle of icy water on my neck or on my back—water that had condensed from the steam and gathered in the wool of my sweater. I would then get up and try to stay warm by walking around. Even then, however, I had to move slowly because the fog was so thick that I could not even see the flow of the pit, and there was no way for me to know exactly where it was.

What is called a sense of direction is not a "sense" in the proper meaning of that term. I think it is actually a kind of special attention that registers, consciously or unconsciously, the parameters of a route in the memory. This information makes it possible for a person to retain an idea of the relationship between his own position and a given point—whether that point be simply north, or, in extraordinary circumstances, a cauldron of boiling lava. I usually have that kind of attention, through no particular effort on my part and even when I don't need it, even though I may be reading, talking, or writing instead of paying attention to landmarks or direction. The misadventure of Ben Bella, who didn't notice when his plane from Spain turned and headed for Algiers when he thought he was going to

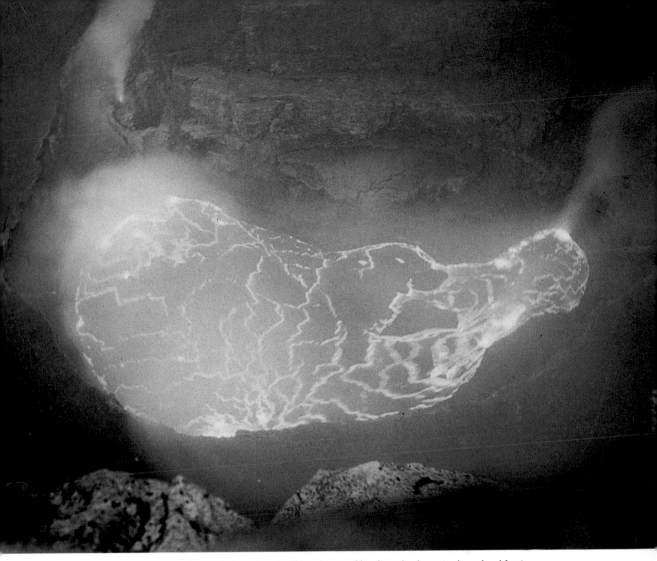

1953. In five years, the lake had shrunk to half its size and had sunk almost a hundred feet.

Cairo, would be very unlikely in my case. Down in the caldera, however, my sense of direction was completely useless. I was a prisoner of the steam, and there was nothing for me to do but sit still and wait for it to clear enough for me to catch sight of the pit. The famous "attention" that I mentioned was not functioning during the hours that I was in the caldera, repeatedly sitting, standing up, trying to move about, lying down over the fissures, and then beginning all over again. My subconscious simply did not register direction. Thus, I was wholly unaware of where north was, where the pit was, and even where the circular wall of my prison was. The relative nearness of the pit and the thickness of the steam condemned me to virtual immobility; and immobility was particularly unpleasant because of the condensation that soaked my clothing.

Then, suddenly, there was a break in the steam. I could make out a bit of starry sky, and I could also see the glow of the pit. I lay on my stomach, my head and shoulders protruding over the edge, and looked down. What I discovered was something that I had never seen before: the breathtaking beauty of a caldera's whole interior at night. The lake of lava was certainly impressive because of its incandescence, which was much more visible in darkness than during daylight when it was more or less veiled by the gray-ish skin of cooling rock at its surface. But what was new to me—and even now, twenty-five years later, the memory is still fresh in my mind—was the spectacular sight of the vertical walls of the caldera illuminated by the reddish glow of the pit which they circumscribed. My eyes drank in the al-ien splendor emanating from those colossal walls on which reds, purples, and shadowy blacks played almost imperceptibly in rhythm with the swell and flow of the golden fountains of molten rock some 600 feet below.

My astonishment mingled with surprise at two things. First, there was the fact that the lake of lava was calm, whereas my memory of it from my first visit was that its surface was broken by "waves" or gigantic bubbles. The second thing was that the lake now occupied a new, smaller bed than it had previously. Five years earlier, the edge of the lake lapped at the walls of the pit. Now, there was a circular ledge or terrace separating it from those same walls. I could only conclude that, in the intervening five years, the lake had shrunk considerably, and that it had sunk perhaps 100 feet.

Then, as suddenly as it had dissipated, the steam was back, and the glow of the pit disappeared. It was as though I had had a dream. I backed away from the edge of the pit and stood facing it. I did an about-face to be cer-tain that the pit was now directly to my rear, and walked away counting my steps. Every six steps, I stopped, bent down, and made a small heap of pebbles—while making sure that I remained facing in the same direction.

The steam cleared momentarily several more times during the night, and each time I repeated the process until, finally, the floor of the terrace was marked by my directional signals: a kind of spiderweb of pebbles radiating from the edge of the pit. There were still traces of the web many years lat-er. That night, it allowed me to move about the floor and to warm myself somewhat without danger of stumbling into the pit, while I waited for a chance to see once more the marvel of those circular walls alive with the eerie glow of the lake of lava. Such precautions may seem excessive, per-haps even laughable. But when people are alone and surrounded by hostile nature, they must operate with extreme prudence. Paradoxically, the more risks they take, the more careful they must be.

Dawn finally came and, simultaneously, the weather cleared. Tormoz and Deru hurried down the wall and brought me something to eat, a Ther-mos of hot tea and—what I wanted most of all—a dry sleeping bag. I re-moved my damp clothing and slid into the heavenly comfort of the bag's

Louis Tormoz at the edge of the pit.

warmth. I was asleep even before Tormoz and Deru began climbing the wall again to bring down the others.

The chief purpose of this visit to the Nyiragongo caldera was to decide on the best spot, and on the proper technique, of climbing down the vertical wall of the pit in order to reach the lava lake itself. During my earlier visit, I had been too preoccupied by our unexpected discovery of the lava lake for me to give much consideration to the problem of getting down that wall which, nonetheless, was the *sine qua non* of any valid research project. The wall in question was quite vertical, with a slight overhang at the top, and with a 650-foot drop. It was composed of successive horizontal layers that appeared cut, as though by a knife of lava ending at the lava lake. For an experienced climber, it was an easy descent because of the abundance of holds on which to rest the edge of one's shoe or the tips of one's fingers. Moreover, there were breaks in the wall formed by dikes, which made the descent easier because the climber could jam an arm, leg, or even an entire body, into them.

I remembered all these things from my first visit, despite the fact that I was somewhat distracted by the sight of the lake itself. That memory led me to believe that there would be no problem in the descent, so long as we

The upper terrace and, 600 feet below, the newborn lower terrace.

were careful to avoid being directly over the lake itself where the heat, even if we used heat-resistant clothing, would be unbearable. Nonetheless, I was wary of trusting too much the first impressions of an apprentice volcanologist, even though the apprentice was myself. My experience since then had taught me that the walls of craters are generally not nearly as solid as they look. They are formed by geological faults and have a covering of unsteady block not yet swept away by erosion. In addition, volcanoes are frequently shaken by earthquakes and by minor, but continual, tremors, which loosen the rock. The holds, therefore, while they might make the descent relatively easy, also make it dangerous.

Since the goals of volcanolgy are different from those of mountain climbing, it is up to the volcanologist to reduce, as much as possible, the risks and efforts required to gather specimens and measurements and to observe the volcano. That consideration made me eliminate the possibility of simply climbing down a rope into the pit, and then climbing up again with the help of hands, elbows, feet, and knees—a *varappe*, as we call it in the Alps. Instead, I decided to use a windlass. I would have to find the right spot to attach it; that is, a spot protected from falling rocks, which are frequent and are dangerous since the cable from which I would be hanging would probably get caught on protruding rocks and ledges.

On this occasion, the continuing bad weather made it impossible for me to examine the entire circumference of the pit's floor. It was all we could do to climb back up to the rim, chilled and empty-handed, before the day ended as it had begun in steam.

On our way back down the mountain, we had an unexpected misadventure. As we trudged down the muddy, slippery trail through the jungle, we heard a sudden and very loud trumpeting that could have come only from one source. Reactions to elephants are an individual thing. Some people fear them, and others do not. The members of our party, both black and white, were rather evenly divided in that respect. I belonged to the group that habitually regarded elephants with respect, but without fear. On this occasion, however, for some reason we were all immediately overcome by panic. I think that the fog was responsible for this extraordinary reaction. Our reaction in the thick fog and the darkness was pretty much the same. We could see nothing, and the sudden, piercing noise—which seemed to come from practically on top of us—sent us all into headlong flight down the mountain. Our attempt to run away, however, was quickly halted by people tripping over vines and falling, slipping in the mud, and running headlong into trees. In retrospect, I don't think that I even realized that the sound I had heard was an elephant's trumpeting until I fell and was on my stomach on the ground, panting with exhaustion as well as terror. For someone who had always prided himself on his "cool," it was a humiliating experience; and the fact that no one else had behaved any better was no consolation to me.

By the time we regained control over our emotions, we realized that all our baggage and equipment had been abandoned in flight. This complicated our situation enormously. We could not use the trail because the elephant that had scared us so much, but for some reason had not pursued us, was now standing across the trail and blocking it. We therefore had to make a detour through thick jungle, without knives or machetes or even flashlights. Everything had been dropped in our panic to get away. I did make a half-hearted attempt to get around the elephant, but a single trumpeting was enough to give wings to my feet and I got away as fast as I could. The two men who tried after me retreated as quickly as they could after having crept close enough to the animal to hear his stomach growling.

In addition to our problems with the jungle as we made our way down the mountain, we were very worried about two of our party whom we had not been able to find after our wild stampede down the slopes. They showed up the following morning, but we had spent the night picturing them being trampled by the elephant. Such things happen too frequently in Africa for anyone to regard it as improbable.

Lake Kivu and its shoreline of basalt.

2

The first scientific expedition: 1958

Preparations

The years passed. My obstinacy, and that of the chief of the Congolese Parks Bureau, remained undiminished. Mine was like that of a spider who, without noticeable discouragement, continues relentlessly to try to climb the sides of a glass jar in which he is trapped. The chief, on the other hand, had only to maintain his veto for Nyiragongo to remain closed to me. By then, I had given up the idea of setting up an observatory on the volcano, not only because I could not even get to Nyiragongo, but also because my plans had evolved.

A safari crossing a recent lava flow from Nyamuragira.

Opposite: Tramping across the savannah toward Nyiragongo, which is the most distant peak. The volcano in front of Nyiragongo is the latter's impressive satellite, Shaheru.

In 1956, it had been six years since we had discovered the fantastic phenomenon of the lava lake. In that time, I had learned many things, not the least of which was the pleasure of being independent. On the other side of the ledger, I had lost much of the somewhat juvenile enthusiasm that had made me want to immure myself in an observatory in the middle of the jungle. It was not that I was any the less excited about the possibility of studying Nyiragongo, but that I had come to realize how sterile such research might be if I remained in that out-of-the-way place, cut off from the mainstream of scientific thought, from contact with my colleagues, and from everything else available—such as universities, lectures, and meetings—in the centers of Western civilization. Also, to confine myself to an observatory on Nyiragongo would be, in effect, to limit my research to a relatively limited sphere. As I learned more and more about my new field of volcanology, I became aware of the complexity of volcanic phenomena. And, at the same time, I began to understand that it would be better for me to be able to make use of a variety of methods and to study volcanism in all its manifestations. Thus, I concluded that it would be a mistake for me to confine myself exclusively to the study of a single volcano, no matter how fascinating that volcano might be. Now, a quarter of a century later, I am convinced that one of the reasons why volcanology had made so little progress until then, was that almost every volcanologist had his own "pet" volcano to which he devoted himself exclusively. Another reason had to do with the obvious insufficiency of means at the disposal of volcanologists. There were practically no funds available, for example, for the study of such difficult problems as there were for those of meteorology or other more "practical" studies.

In 1958, ten years after the discovery of Nyiragongo's lake, I was finally able to organize a scientific expedition. Its objective was twofold: to take samples of the molten lava and of the gases emanating from the lava, and to gather as much data as possible on the various phenomena within the caldera.

I will not dwell on the difficulty of securing the necessary permits and authorizations for this expedition. Suffice it to say that if I had not had sufficient determination, I would have given up the idea of an expedition long before ten years had passed. After all, although a permanent lake of lava may be the ideal place to study eruptions, there are enough volcanoes other than Nyiragongo to keep a volcanologist busy. The thing about Nyiragongo was that it was a challenge, not only *qua* volcano but also *qua* challenge. For the same reason, I like mountain climbing, boxing, racing,

Opposite, above: Our camp on the rim of the caldera.

Opposite, below: A rock-fall along the interior wall.

rugby, and chess—because they are challenges. I was absolutely determined to do everything I could to move the proper pieces on the politico-scientific chessboard until I achieved the checkmate that would cause the doors of Nyiragongo to swing open. In this case, the checkmate took the form of intervention by Leopold III, king of the Belgians and friend of naturalists and scientists. Whereupon, I immediately set to work organizing my expedition.

The most important consideration in any expedition, it seems to me, is security or safety. Regardless of an expedition's importance or goals, the primary responsibility of the organizer is to get his people back alive and in one piece. Next, in my hierarchy of values, comes the necessity of gathering as much scientific data as is humanly possible. Those two considerations make it necessary for me to choose the members of an expedition on the basis of three factors: security, knowledge, and sociability. Then, once I have chosen my associates, I turn over to them the various areas of responsibility in the organization of the expedition itself: organization, authorizations and permits, transportation, logistics, equipment, etc. Meanwhile, I coordinate all these activities so that there will be no unpleasant surprises before or during the expedition.

This rather pragmatic approach to expeditions has evolved over the years, and it has worked for me. In 1958, however, it was not nearly so clear in my mind because I had not yet had as much experience as I have now. And that expedition was fairly large, comprising a dozen scientists and, in addition, a certain number of necessary technical assistants. Moreover, Nyiragongo was not Etna or Stromboli, which are the most accessible of the volcanoes since they are in the middle of Mediterranean civilization. Even at a time when colonialism tended to facilitate such matters, Nyiragongo was hardly accessible. It was situated in the heart of deepest Africa, a day's march from Goma, which was the closest place from which one could obtain medical, mechanical, or simply human help.

Opposite, upper left: Professor Ivan de Magnée and Major Tulpin on the wall.

Opposite, upper right: Professor de Magnée with his Geiger counter.

Opposite, below: Our camp at the foot of the debris along the southern wall.

The lower terrace, although still quite new, was already littered with countless rocks fallen from the fragile wall above.

Opposite: There were formidable crevices near the pit.

Our camp in the caldera, seen from the rim.

Fortunately, I had the support of my friend Professor Ivan de Magnée, from the beginning of the adventure to the end of it. I left to him the choice of the participants, the organization of the scientific program, and the contact with the authorities. In fact, I asked him to become the official head of the expedition. Now that permission to go to Nyiragongo had finally been obtained, I thought it expedient to keep a low profile so as not to irritate the Congolese authorities more than I already had. They were still omnipotent in Virunga National Park to which we were going. Moreover, this arrangement relieved me of the responsibility for such chores as visits of protocol and other formalities, and left me free to concentrate on what was really important: security.

Now that the possibility of an expedition to Nyiragongo had been translated from dream into actuality, the unruffled certitude that I had felt concerning the feasibility of the undertaking began to give way to creeping uncertainty. I had always visualized the expedition as comprising a tightly knit group of men experienced in such enterprises, with whom a descent to the lava lake would present no particular danger. Instead of a homogeneous little team, however, we were going to be a group of about twenty, only two of whom were experienced climbers. This meant that eighteen of our party, regardless of their qualifications in other areas, would run considerable risk in the descent because of excess apprehension or audacity.

The selection of one's companions on an adventure such as this is of utmost importance. I have learned through experience that the primary criterion is not, as I thought for so many years, a person's scientific credentials or passion for research. That is secondary. In first place are those traits of character that make a person an agreeable companion. The characteristic to guard against most when choosing associates for an expedition is *egotism*. As a member of a team, a person must think of others and of the team first. When all members of a team think in that fashion, no individual has to worry about his or her own welfare because all the others worry about it as well. But, as I've said, in 1958 I didn't have the experience that I have today; at that time, I still thought that knowledge was more important than wisdom. It was not until the mid-sixties, when we were making frequent trips to Etna, that we learned to apply a simple test to judge the team spirit of new members. Every evening, the various pieces of equipment and supplies that we needed for the next day's trek to the erupting crater were lined up along the path. Then, before setting out in the morning, everyone was expected to take one of the loads and carry it up to the volcano. Invariably, the good team members would unhesitatingly select the heaviest or most cumbersome loads. We knew we had a perfect team when the smallest and lightest loads were the last ones taken.

Generally, the longer and harder the mission, the more essential it is that the members of an expedition be a real team. This is particularly true in polar expeditions. Unfortunately, the larger the expedition, the more difficult it is to achieve this homogeneity. On the other hand, the size of an expedition has a direct bearing on the amount of scientific data that can be gathered. Thus, there exists an intrinsic contradiction that every organizer of an expedition must resolve.

Finally, thanks above all to Ivan de Magnée, everything was ready. He had recruited our scientists, and he had made the mandatory protocol visits both in Europe and after our arrival in the Congo. We were ready to start work. I had the added pleasure of once more being in familiar territory. I found Lake Kivu, with its mountainous peninsulas and verdant

Our winch apparatus was installed only a few feet from the edge of the caldera.

shores, as beautiful as ever. And with a stab of joy I recognized the familiar but forgotten smell of the African bush—a sharp odor combining the smells of brush fires, villages, smoke from wood fires, fermented banana juice, jasmine, and human sweat. To these were added the indefinable and almost intoxicating scents that seem to rise only at night.

A team of researchers

It took over two days for our entire party to reach the rim of Nyiragongo. Kibati, the village where the trail began, was about six miles from the summit. The party participants and the bearers who were to carry our

We double-checked and tested everything before beginning work.

equipment and supplies to the rim of the caldera were so numerous that the group spread out over that entire distance. The truth was that our scientists' legs were in no better shape than their lungs, and the length of our caravan reflected the slowness with which they moved. Several of our experts even had to stop at the Bruyeres camp overnight (at an altitude of 9,600 feet) and wait until the next morning to climb the remaining 1,400 feet.

The first camp—camp number one, we called it—was established at the rim. Camille Tulpin, a major in the Congolese army, had already arrived with the detachment of soldiers who were to relieve us of logistic worries. This kind of cooperation is important on expeditions where it is necessary to provide food, shelter, and the opportunity of working in peace to a group of people who have ventured out into a world which, to them at least, is alien and hostile. There are a hundred things to be taken care of: transportation of equipment and supplies, pitching and maintenance of the camp, food and water, heat, light, telecommunications, sanitary facilities—the list is unending. Major Tulpin took over these responsibilities without a moment's hesitation. His sense of order, his energy, his tactful but perfect control over his own men and over the bearers was such that he remains in my mind as the exemplar of everything that such a commander should be. He even looked the part, being a burly, gnarled man with a strong chin and a blond handlebar mustache that had earned him the nickname of "Mylord." The major's interests in life, not necessarily in order of preference, were big game hunting (such game was plentiful in this area), attractive women, and physical obstacles against which to pit his endurance and strength. The idea of going down into the crater of an active volcano was his cup of tea; he had the advantage over me of being intrigued, rather than worried, by the fact that the vast majority of our party had never done any climbing before.

Despite my worries, I tried to approach this problem with as much patience and attention as the major did. I was concerned above all that one of our neophytes might have an accident. The fact that the interior wall of the caldera was vertical—the primary concern of those who have never climbed—was not what bothered me. Instead, I was worried about two things. First, the abundance of loose rocks and insecure holds jutting out from the wall; and, second, that our beginners, after they had gotten used to the idea of verticality, would take it too casually. A vertical cliff is very impressive when you first look at it. But, if it has places on which to get a hand- or foot-hold, it is not nearly so frightening. I was afraid that, once they had physically and psychologically accepted the fact that such a wall is hardly more difficult to climb than any other slope, they would lose their caution completely. I have seen beginning climbers do things that made my hair stand on end. In this case, Tulpin and I began by taking down one "pupil" at a time. With the major in front and me behind, we carefully guided him down the 650 feet of wall. The second stage was for us to take down two beginners at a time. Finally, we were satisfied that everyone knew what they were doing.

We pitched a second camp on the floor of the terrace at the foot of a large pile of blocks resulting from the collapse of a section of wall. Such collapses are one of the principal dangers within a crater, and they occur rather frequently because the walls are often shaken by tremors. A good strong tremor is all that it takes to send a couple of tons of debris from a weakened wall crashing down to the floor of the caldera. We've never had an accident of this kind, even though we've spent several weeks at a stretch inside craters, but I must say that I am much more conscious of this danger than I am of the possibility of a sudden eruption.

The geophysicists and geologists in our party got to work immediately. I had told them about the lake, of course, but the reality of the spectacle surpassed my description.

No one was disappointed, or indifferent to this example of nature's marvels.

In his role as head of the expedition, Professor de Magnée saw to the launching of the various research projects. He prospected the terrain for radioactivity with a Geiger counter, since the proportion of radon or thoron produced by radioactive minerals contained in the rocks can provide data on variations in the flow of volcanic material. Meanwhile, the geophysicists were taking their seismic readings and their measurements, while the geologists took rock samples from the successive strata lining the upper wall.

Operation windlass

During a hurried visit in 1953, I was surprised to see that the lake, which had been so large only five years before, had both shrunk and sunk, thereby exposing a new ring-shaped terrace. Now, five more years had passed, and it was immediately obvious that the level of the lake had sunk once more. As a result, there were now three levels. Seen from the rim of the crater, the vertical wall to the third level was concentrically surrounded by the evidence of the first. This latest level seemed to be eighty to one hundred feet down. The drop in level came as a complete surprise to me, and left me somewhat perplexed.

Finally, I decided that I would worry about the third level when we came to it. First, we had to descend to the second level. The general opinion among those who knew volcanoes was that such a descent was, if not impossible, at least extremely dangerous. In any event, since the lake was uninhabitable because of the heat and the gases, it was too risky for any in-depth scientific study to be conducted there. My own experience with volcanoes led me to a contrary opinion; it remained to be seen who was right. Nonetheless, after years of being told that the project was impossible, I had begun to have a few vague doubts of my own.

Ten years earlier, when I first saw the lava lake, I had no difficulty in devising various ways of reaching it: climbing down a rope; using a rope ladder; using a winch or windlass operated by someone who remained above, in which case the person actually making the descent would be suspended from the end of a steel cable. Most of the time, I imagined the descent to be more or less a solo undertaking—climbing down a rope, and then scaling the wall (the *varappe*) to get back to the top. This meant that anyone working with me would necessarily have been someone experienced in acrobatics of this kind. As things turned out, most of the party actually knew nothing about climbing, and so we had to devise some kind of elevator to get them up and down. The kind of elevator that I had in mind was a windlass. This involved fairly heavy equipment, slow movement, and communication difficulties between the operators of the windlass and the climber being lowered or raised. But, since we were working with neophytes, we had to do everything possible to reduce the element of risk.

Our first job was to find the proper spot to set up the windlass. There were two factors in our choice. They were both negative factors, but imperative nonetheless. To begin with, the windlass could not be located in a spot where the explorer would hang directly over the lake of molten lava—which, at that time, lay in the southern quarter of the pit. Also, we would have to avoid areas with many fissures; otherwise, not only might the cable loosen rocks that would then fall on the explorer, but a section of the wall itself might crumble if there were a tremor. After much examination of terrain and many discussions, we concluded that there was really no ideal spot to install our windlass. That being the case, we ended up choosing the least unfavorable site, which lay on the north side of the caldera. It had crevasses, but they were concentric and rather small and not very numerous. The interior wall of the caldera that could be reached from that spot was relatively clean; that is, it had few projections, ledges, etc. (and it was sufficiently removed from the lake itself to be safe. It took us an entire day to select the site, and another day to transport the needed equipment from our main camp to this spot. Then, finally, we were able to set up the windlass.

There were two problems having to do with the fragility of the wall. There was the danger to the men going down into the caldera and then coming up to the rim again. But there was also the risk involved for the team operating the windlass; that is, the two men working the cranks and

The very rare lava of Nyiragongo, with its nests of leucite, nepheline, and melilite.

the third man on the telephone. In order to reduce any risk that the rim of the caldera might crumble and send them all down to the caldera floor we tried to locate the windlass about twenty feet back from the rim and to re- lay the cable into the caldera by means of a kind of spar or bowsprit: a moveable arm projecting from the windlass. The arm would be able to turn on a vertical axis attached to a Duralumin prop which would give stability to the apparatus. The arm's turning motion would enable us to move the explorer over the rim, and later to bring him back, without his having to scramble over the top. It took us several days to rig up this apparatus. To keep it from moving, we anchored it solidly with steel guys which, in turn, we attached to steel rods inserted into cracks in the rock. Then we piled rocks around its base. Once the windlass had been bolted onto the arm, we strung the cable from its spool aroung the pulley located at the end of the arm and, finally, we secured the ring, at the end of the cable, from which we would hang as we took turns going down.

We took the greatest care throughout this whole operation. Accidents do happen in speleological expeditions, in mountain climbing, in explora- tions of deserts, jungles, polar regions, and active volcanoes. That is more or less in the order of things, and the element of risk that a participant ac- cepts adds spice to the adventure. It is the responsibility of heads of expeditions, however, to keep that risk to an acceptable minimum. Since it is impossible for any human being to foresee absolutely everything that may happen, the chief's next responsibility is to react quickly and appro- priately when something does go wrong. After all, the possibility of acci- dents is an integral part of any expedition, and heads of the expeditions have met these responsibilities if they have taken all necessary precau- tions beforehand, and if they keep their heads when an accident does oc- cur. And, finally, if there is an accident, they should be willing to accept and to admit whatever responsibility they had for it.

The memory of a past accident was present, very much present, in my mind while Mylord Tulpin and I, with the help of four soldiers and of our factotum, Louis Couteller—who fortunately had nothing else to do—set up our windlass at the rim of Nyiragongo's caldera. When it came time to loop the end of the cable, we secured the loop with triple bindings, and then checked it and re-checked it until even I felt that perhaps we were go- ing overboard.

For the past several days, I had been sleeping badly. Alone at night, the day's work done and the discussions finished, I was haunted by the unease, the touch of inquietude, that had gnawed at me from the moment that the final decision to mount the expedition had been taken. It was a feeling that I had never experienced before. Until then, I had merely accepted danger as part of the game and put it out of my mind, at least to the extent that I did not worry about it. I, like every other human being, was absolutely convinced of my own immortality. Or, at least I believed that if I did die, it would only be after an endless span of years that lay between me and old age. I still believe that, of course; but what has changed is that, as soon as I assumed responsibility for other people, I lost not only the freedom that working alone confers, but also the laissez-faire attitude that had characterized my outlook. Some members of our expedition had volunteered to accompany me purely because of their interest in Nyiragongo. But there were others whom I had actively persuaded by promising them a practically virgin field of scientific research. These people I felt obliged to look after as a mountain guide looks after his charges. That sense of being responsible for others is hard to bear, especially at night, and my imagination ran wild as soon as I slipped into my sleeping bag.

Sleeping bags, by the way, were by no means an unnecessary luxury on the slopes of this equatorial volcano, where the humidity and the cold combine to turn the rain into sleet. The sleet, in turn, covered our dark mineral surroundings with a white powder that seemed alien to the gray clouds and the smoke rising from the caldera. The clouds themselves sometimes went down into the caldera. We could see them float over the circular crest, then drift downward into the caldera like waterfalls in slow motion. Sometimes they dissipated as they reached the opening; sometimes they also spread out along the ground, enveloping us in their thick fog. I knew from experience how annoying such fogs could be. There were times when they remained for hours, bringing all work to a halt and making it dangerous even to move about because of the poor visibility.

The descent into hell

Finally, the windlass was assembled, thoroughly checked, and declared operational. It was time for the first descent.

I decided that I was going to go first. I would be the guinea pig, but I would also be the beneficiary. My motives were not altogether altruistic. It was true that I could not very well ask someone else to be the first to ex-

The second wall seen from below during the first descent. Note the marker protruding above the pit's edge.

Tulpin goes down.

pose himself to the risks that might be involved, but it was also true that I did not want to leave to anyone else the subtle but intoxicating pleasure of being the first to reach the bottom of the pit.

I do not recall having felt any particular emotion as I found myself hanging in midair over the pit. I had done it before, testing the windlass. This time, it was for real, but I had absolute confidence in the apparatus, which had been built by a friend who was an engineer specializing in such machines. What I do recall was my full appreciation of being at the starting point of an unprecedented exploration.

An athlete is accustomed to being a winner; that is, to being first, to do something or get somewhere before anyone else. The better an athlete is, the less arrogant he or she is about the idea of being first. Excellence, it seems, goes hand in hand with respect for the abilities of others. Often the most talented people in sports are the most modest. This does not mean that they are without the fierce pride that makes it possible to win. Pride is totally different from vanity. I hate vanity, and when I see signs of it in myself I react with anger and disgust. I had a little discussion with myself on the subject as I was being lowered into the crater: "If no one was watching me," I asked myself, "and no one even knew that I was here, would I enjoy this as much?"

The fact that I asked myself the question was enough to reassure me. Without worrying anymore about my motives, I relaxed and let myself enjoy one of the rarest experiences: to be able to set foot where no one has ever walked before. I knew that I would have felt the same pleasure—or even more intense pleasure—if I had been all alone on Nyiragongo. In fact, I even experienced a twinge of nostalgic regret for an old dream: to be alone in the caldera, truly alone, more alone than I had been in 1953 when my companions spent the night hanging in the fog, alongside the interior wall of the caldera.

Soon, I had no more time for psychological speculation. I had now come level with the bottom of a flexible metal ladder hanging from the rim of the caldera. The mania for precautions that I had made me devise an alternative method of climbing out of the caldera. If the windlass stopped working for some reason, we would use speleological ladders to get out, instead of taking the risks involved in trying to scale the vertical wall with its undependable holds. We had attached the top of this ladder as solidly as we could to a steel bar inserted into a crack in the solid rock that was the "ground" surrounding the rim. It was my job to lengthen the ladder on my way down by adding additional thirty-foot sections. A large bag containing

Our bivouac on the lower level.

Opposite: Tulpin at the edge of the pit.

Exploring the lower level.

twenty of these sections, each one rolled into a lightweight cylinder, was riding down with me at the end of the cable. I was supposed to give the "stop" order by telephone (there was a spool feeding out telephone wire as I went down). Then I would take a ladder from the bag, unroll it, and attach it to the ladder above by means of special rings. (They were extremely functional ladders, lightweight, made of thin steel cables with aluminum treads, and relatively easy to handle.) Then I would signal for the descent to continue.

At the beginning of the descent, I was in midair, several yards away from the nearest wall. But I soon reached the point where I was able to prop myself against the wall, first with the tips of my shoes and then with the entire length of the soles. This was a much more comfortable arrangement. We were using a nonrotating cable on the windlass, but there was still a slight tendency for the cable to twist. If the cable twisted, then not only the suspension cable itself twisted, but also the telephone wire and a second steel cable that we were going to use to raise and lower supplies and equipment also twisted. From the psychological standpoint, it was much more reassuring to have my feet on solid ground—even though it was vertical—than to have them hanging in the air. Moreover, this sort of contact made it possible for me to bear slightly to the right or to the left when necessary.

The descent progressed slowly. For reasons of security, the windlass could not lower a person at a rate more than four or five yards a minute. I occupied my time in disposing of loose stones and rocks on the face of the wall by working them loose and letting them fall. Thus, I hoped, I was lessening the danger of such debris falling while we were working below. At the same time, I was examining the composition of the wall.

Obviously, it was not a question of identifying the different kinds of rock in each layer. The problem with lava (which, by definition, is magma that has reached the surface and has "hardened" upon contact with the air) is that a high percentage of it is vitreous or noncrystalline, which means that its composition is not immediately obvious and must be determined by chemical analysis. Rough-grained rocks, which have cooled very slowly under the surface, and the minerals in them form crystals that are easily recognizable, either with the naked eye or with the help of a magnifying glass. The shape and cut of those crystals make it possible to identify the minerals in the rock. With some volcanic rock, however, one can draw only approximate (and often erroneous) conclusions. Moreover, I am not an expert mineralogist, and I would never dare to identify a specimen of lava. What I was trying to do was to distingush the various strata, with respect either to the presence or absence of crystalline mineral. I must say that the lavas of Nyiragongo are not by any means ordinary. I might even say that they are exceptional. There are thousands of volcanoes located either on the continents or beneath the sea, most of which straddle the boundaries of two tectonic plates in the process of moving apart from one another. These are referred to as ridge volcanoes and they tend to be effusive or emit lava from a vent or fissure deep beneath the earth's surface. The magma of these volcanoes is primarily basalt—a rock that underlies all the continents and ocean bottoms. The mineral composition of basalt varies, however, depending upon other liquids it combines with, and how fast it cools. Since the mineral composition of the magma is always different, when it cools, the resulting rocks are also different, although closely related. Most often, the basalt may contain more or less quartz, alkaline feldspar, and olivine.

There are also volcanoes located along the edges of the earth's tectonic plates at points where the plates are colliding with one another. These are referred to as arc volcanoes and they tend to be explosive. The explosions produce mostly ash, pyroclastic bombs, and steam. The lava tends to be rich in quartz and very viscous. The rock is usually rhyolite, trachyte, phonolite, and andesite.

Nyiragongo, like that of the entire Virunga chain, is neither of these types because it is situated in the East African Rift valley. This valley is spreading apart and may eventually mark the point where two tectonic plates are separating. Nyiragongo's lava differs from all known lavas to such a degree that it has been given a name of its own: niligongite (from *Niligongo*, a variant of Nyiragongo). It is perhaps difficult to defend this custom of coining a new name every time the chemical composition of a substance varies slightly from the norm. It has been the custom to derive a name for a rock from the name of the place where it is found. Some specialists have now begun to adopt the method of using a family name coupled with a more specific name.

Niligongite, in fact, is nothing more than the rock nephelinite containing the minerals leucite and melilite. The primary mineral in nephelinite is nepheline, an uncommon mineral. Leucite is another mineral not commonly encountered, and melilite is even rarer. A rock containing all three is truly out of the ordinary, but that is no reason to make up a new name for it.

Nyiragongo is not made up of only nephelinite containing leucite and melilite. Its other rocks are melilite containing leucite, or leucitite containing nepheline. Those three componenets are constant, and geologists who are not specialists in petrography say that we are splitting hairs in distinguishing among the rocks. Be that as it may, all these rocks are unusually poor in silica, the reasons for which are as yet unexplained. Is it a basalt,

Opposite, above: Tulpin at the edge of the second level.

Opposite, below: A view from the second level.

Below: The floating island and the lava lake.

normal in origin but transformed by a loss of silica but a gain in alkaline elements through the absorption of other rocks encountered in its rise from the depths? Or is it a magma that was exceptional even in its origins, either nephelinic or carbonic?

To ask such a question is not to split hairs. Indeed, it is a very important question, not only if we are better to understand the origins and evolutions of the earth, but also to understand the origins of certain kinds of mineral lodes. The time is coming when all such known lodes will be exhausted, and new ones will have to be prospected, at increasingly greater depths. Since a good number of these lodes are more or less connected with volcanic phenomena, it will be necessary to understand the nature, workings, and effects of the latter if such prospecting is to be efficient and economical.

That having been said, I should add that such considerations were far from my mind as I continued my slow descent into the caldera of Nyiragongo. My eyes continued to move from left to right and then from right to left again at each new layer, searching for characteristic crystals and, even more, for some fragment of rock carried up from a deeper layer of nonvolcanic rock (that is, from the rock underlying the volcano) through which the magma had risen before reaching the surface. Such specimens, possibly melted upon contact with magma, can provide the interesting data on the rock underlying the volcano, on the depth of its source, and on the origin of its lava. However, I did not see a single such piece of evidence in the wall with its hundred or so horizontal strata. It is true that I was busy with other problems as well. For example, I had to work my feet frantically against the wall to keep myself facing always in the same direction. That was the main problem in my descent. Extending the speleological ladder presented no special difficulty. I did, however, have a tendency to turn in midair whenever my feet lost contact with the wall, as they did when, for example, I finished "walking" over a projection and momentarily hung in midair. The problem at that point was to keep the cables and wires from twisting—no small feat when you consider the number of them that I had to keep separated.

The lower part of the wall was not vertical, and so I was delighted to reach it. First of all, I could almost stand upright. And second, I knew then that I was on the second leg of my downward journey. Unless you've been through it, you have no idea of how simultaneously satisfying and uncomfortable it is to regain the use of your feet after spending an hour or so hanging in the air. It's satisfying because you're capable of independent action again; and uncomfortable because, by then, your legs are stiff and numb. I had to wait several minutes before the circulation in my legs was normal again. Then, it took another few minutes, with my back to the wall, the foot of which was only at a 60° angle, before I reached the floor of the terrace.

There was too much to do for me to take great pleasure in having reached that point, or to abandon myself to psychological speculation again. First, I had to secure the end of the slender cable that we were going to use to ferry supplies and equipment from the rim. Immediately after securing the cable to a rock, I turned my attention to the next job: guiding the windlass cable back to the rim of the caldera with the help of a 200-yard cord, so that it would not get stuck on a projection or in a crevice.

Tulpin then sent down a tent, food, an oxygen tank, a supply of filters for gas masks, geophones, a pyroscope, and some cameras. Next, he came down himself, stopping only once en route: at about seventy-five feet above the floor, so as to attach a strong rope, easy to grip, to the bottom of the last section of ladder I had installed. We needed twenty sections of ladder to reach the bottom, and I had had only seventeen. The other three had to be secured to a vertical strip on the upper wall in order to make the strip easier for the less skillful to negotiate.

Mylord was unabashedly delighted to be down and was bursting with energy. His Flemmish accent rolled out from between the equally prominent chin and mustache. He shook himself like a dog just out of the water and, with gestures as voluble as his speech, he worked to restore circulation to his long, muscular legs and arms.

We were windward of the lake, but we heard its noise from where we were standing. The air, though hardly pure, was quite breathable. Indeed, I would have gladly breathed much worse air for the sake of being there. As it was, in the three hours that I had been in the caldera, I had felt no need for a gas mask.

Mylord and I pitched our tent and put our supplies and equipment in order before having a bite to eat. Then I made my report, by telephone, to Ivan de Magnée. It was a pleasure to hear his voice, particularly since I could tell how pleased he was at the good news from within the caldera. Unfortunately, he, in turn, had a bit of bad news to communicate: the official geologist of the National Parks Bureau had showed up and was demanding to be lowered to the terrace of the caldera. At Professor de Magnée's insistence, I agreed to this somewhat unwise demand.

I was unhappy about it for two reasons. First, I wanted men around me

The fissures in the terrace precede a collapse of part of the wall.

Opposite: The southern tip of the lava lake and the floating island.

of whom I felt sure, both as climbers and as dependable companions. The second reason was my personal antipathy for the person in question. But, since I had no real choice in the matter, I consented.

It was already past five o'clock in the afternoon and it would soon be dark. Tulpin and I made a quick reconnaissance of the floor to both east and west. The ground was littered with sharp-edged rocks, some of them over six feet in diameter. Even the smaller ones served as a reminder, if we needed one, that the wall encircling us was not nearly as solid as it appeared and that we would have to proceed with caution.

The level we were at, like the lower level, had been cut by the lava lake, as though by a giant cookie cutter. The caldera had been formed, by a sudden collapse of the entire center part of the crater—probably following an equally sudden decrease in magma. Peering over the edge of the terrace into the pit, we could see the wall falling vertically for about sixty-five feet and ending at a section of floating rock, which covered the north-eastern two-thirds of the lake. This island of rock had not changed since we had first seen it ten years before, except that it had pitched at a greater angle as it followed the lake in its sinking movement. As daylight faded, the lake was hidden by those enormous blocks of rock, but we could see the reddish glow of it on the far side of the caldera. We hurried impatiently to see it before darkness fell.

The appearance of molten lava is most spectacular at dusk, when the glare of the sunlight is gone but the darkness has not yet hidden the rim around the lava lake. This was now a gigantic liquid crescent of fire less than a hundred feet from us. It was a lake whose enchanted appearance fascinated us: we were aware of its nature, we knew its composition and scientific formulation, but its supernatural beauty emptied our minds of any other consideration.

The lake was as calm as it had been during my first visit. Yet, seen from close up, its surface displayed a surprising wealth of movement. From the level above, we had seen its geyserlike bubbling, the massive movement that occasionally stirred two-thirds of the visible surface to shift from north to south. From our present vantage point, what we saw was less massive, but no less spellbinding: swells, wavelets, ripples of less impressive size but nonetheless charged with mystery, shivers like the movement of living flesh, cracks that suddenly widened and lengthened in the epidermis of plastic rock to reveal the glowing substance underneath.

We spent hours contemplating a spectacle that is impossible to describe and then doing what we had come to do: measuring temperatures, taking samples, listening through the geophones, observing the activity of the lava. Finally, at three o'clock in the morning, exhaustion descended on us like snow sliding off a pitched roof. We dragged ourselves back to the tent, only to find that we had no sleeping bags. Our companions above had neglected to send them down to us, and we had not previously noticed. The wet of the night was disagreeably cold and damp.

The following morning, after a telephone conversation with the camp and a hot breakfast, which was sent down to us by means of the supply cable, we set out on a tour of the world enclosed within these concentric caldera walls to see what we could find, examine, measure, pick up. . . . When we reached the area to the west of the pit, we were suddenly seized by near-panic. The sulphurous fumes from the pit, which rose there and spread on this level before rising toward the caldera's opening, were so thick and concentrated that our eyes and lungs burned like fire. We stumbled backward and put on the gas masks that we carried, hanging on our chests. Then, once the pain had subsided and we felt adequately protected, we moved forward again—very timidly, to be sure.

The masks were most effective. The purity of the filtered air that I was breathing as we walked through the thick fumes made me realize how bad the air actually was that we had been breathing since yesterday. It was very likely that the quantity of carbon dioxide and suphur dioxide that we had inhaled was beyond the tolerable limit—which explained why Mylord and I, both of whom were inured to physical hardship, had been so exhausted. We decided to continue using the masks.

I was very impressed at the sight of a large rock fragment that had fallen from the wall above, a few feet from the edge of the pit. It was coated with a layer of lava about half an inch thick. The ripples in it left no doubt as to the fact that the lava was once liquid. An enormous wave of very fluid lava had risen and then fallen at that spot when the level of the lake was higher than at present. The rock vividly represented two perils that we had to be on guard against: falling rocks and large splashes of lava. A third—gas— we had already experienced.

There was still a sixty-five-foot drop down to the floating island of rock. Once we had negotiated that drop, there would be any number of ways for us to get to the edge of the lava lake. At first, we intended to climb down by rope, which is child's play for an experienced climber; climbing back up would be only slightly more difficult because of the abundance of fissures and holds in the wall. But, after much discussion, I decided not to use that method. It is true that it would have been very easy for Mylord and me, but I had to think about the other members of our party, and it seemed to me that it would have been risky for them. Moreover, both Mylord and I were suffering from fatigue. No doubt, the bad air was having its effect on us, as was the tension that always accompanies any venture of this sort.

The first harvest

The expedition down into Nyiragongo's caldera was comparatively short of money, men, and equipment. Yet, it bore a harvest of results of which Ivan de Magnée could have been quite proud.

We took many temperature readings. These were taken at a distance, with the optical pyrometer, and the readings were between 1,020°C and 1,095°C (1,868°F and 2,003°F). This was more than 100° Centigrade (over 200° Fahrenheit) higher than the temperature readings taken at the summit

The eruption of Kitsimbanyi on the northern flank of Nyiragongo, seen from a distance of about nine miles.

Opposite, below: The cone of Kitsimbanyi, three days after its birth.

some 600 feet above. The difference is accounted for by the absorption of some of the radiated heat by gases and by the atmospheric humidity.

Edouard Berg, a member of the expedition, had computed the geomagnetic reading of the volcano through a series of measurements. He took these measurements or readings at about 130 different stations on the floor of the first level and found an extremely wide variance among these stations: from +17,400 gammas to −12,800 gammas.

Seismographic sounding, which in this case was used above all for regis-

tering microseismic tremors in the vicinity of the volcano, suffered because of the poverty of our instruments—which is to say that it suffered simply from our poverty. That was unfortunate because studying the variations in intensity and frequency of these tremors would have been a means of gathering precise data on their relationship to the activity of the lava lake; those data would have been the basis for further information.

Radioactivity was carefully measured by Geiger counter, both at the many steam-producing fissures at the rim and at the inactive fissures. There were no abnormal readings which, in itself, is a finding of a kind.

Petrology, which is the microscopic and chemical study of rocks, was the branch of science our expedition contributed to most. This was due especially to the samples gathered from the wall of the caldera. The wall represented a total height of about 1,200 feet, composed entirely of successive strata. These strata were at an angle in the upper wall, and were horizontal in the lower. In both cases, they were the result of successive lava flows, one on top of the other. Those visible on the upper wall are lava that flowed out at the surface and thus served to build up Nyiragongo's impressive cone—a cone that was over 13,000 feet high before its neck collapsed into the magma reservoir to form the present-day caldera. The lava flowed down the slopes of the volcano before solidifying and hardened, layer upon layer at a slant of from 25 to 35 degrees. The collapse of the volcano's neck cut away the uppermost part of these strata.

The wall at the second terrace is also the result of several collapses that were less massive than that at the first level. The latter collapses exposed horizontal strata. These layers of rock were lava intrusions from the lake during periods when the level was rising. Now it was evident that the lake was in a receding phase. During the visits made to Nyiragongo between 1948 and 1958, I had noted a total drop of over 150 feet. In the last year alone, it had fallen almost seventy feet.

These variations in the level of the lake are not easy to understand. In the fourteen days that we had already been in the caldera, we had noticed (at least, we noticed whenever the weather was good enough to allow observation) much more rapid but less ample fluctuations: the level of the lake would rise or fall between three and six feet in just a few minutes. When the lake was at its lowest level, we noticed two narrow, solid surfaces, like two small islands, near the southern end of the lake.

Kitsimbanyi pours out a torrent of molten basalt mixed with scoria.

The samplings of the rock strata were later used by Thure Sahama, a Finnish mineralogist of international renown, to construct a history of the chemical fluctuations that characterized the magma of Nyiragongo. In addition to the samplings, we also found fragments of spongy white rock on the floor of the second level. These samples were a surprise since most volcanic rock is black and gray. These fragments were covered with a layer of recent lava and we concluded that they had been carried up from the magma reservoir many thousands of feet below. The lava, in its upward thrust, had torn loose pieces from a vein of quartz or of granite, had melted them and, at the same time by its heat, had freed the gases within. The bubbling gases, in turn, had transformed the quartz or granite into these foamlike fragments of rock.

While we were in the caldera of Nyiragongo, there was an eruption on the north slope of a neighboring volcano Nyamuragira, about fifteen miles away. It was the seventh eruption in the sixty-five years of the recorded history of the Kivu district. (The eighth would take place in 1966; the ninth, in 1971.) On August 8, 1958, two days before our descent to the second level of Nyiragongo, Kitsimbanyi erupted, and streams of lava poured downhill, running to a distance of twelve miles from their source and covering some 15,000 acres of forest and meadow in just a few weeks.

In our tents at night, we spent countless hours discussing whether or not there was a connection between that eruption and the lessened activity of Nyiragongo, as manifested in the lowered level of the lake. Personally, I did not believe that the two phenomena were related. My experience with eruptions led me to believe that molten rock is too viscous to respond so quickly. The general rule is that two neighboring craters in eruption, even though separated only by a wall a few yards thick, are independent of one another with separate reservoirs of magma. I had seen that rule confirmed often at Kituro, Etna, Stromboli, and Izalco. It was difficult for me to imagine that there could be subterranean tunnels with hydraulic action between two volcanoes fifteen miles apart. I was strengthened in this belief by the fact that Nyiragongo's magma, although belonging to the same family of rocks poor in silica and rich in alkali, was quite different from that of Nyamuragira.

Professor de Magnée, on the other hand, did not reject the hypothesis that the two volcanoes might be fed from the same source. This source would have to be extremely large and deep. Moreover, it would have to be capable of producing two chemically different,though related, magmas—a phenomenon made possible by partial crystallization and, subsequently, by a very low degree of intermixture among the liquid silicates. In this case, the rise of magma in one place would necessitate the fall of the magma level in another place because of hydrostatic balance. In other words, while Nyamuragira was engaged in a spectacular eruption, Nyiragongo would be dormant, its great lake of 1948 now calm and gradually sinking into ever-smaller beds. Or else, the eruption, at an altitude of over 5,000 feet was causing a decrease in pressure in the common reservoir, which, in turn, affected Nyiragongo's lava lake. I did not believe a word of it.

Double page following: The gaps in Kitsimbanyi's circular cone.

3

On the shores of the lake of lava: 1959

Camp number two

In 1959, the team that assembled in camp number two on the terrace of Nyiragongo's caldera was larger than it had been in the preceding year. Major Tulpin once more was my strong right arm for logistical support, but this time he had brought a second-in-command, Lieutenant Defreyne, and six soldiers who had volunteered for the assignment. In addition, I had acquired two other aides for him who were both old friends of mine: Louis Tormoz, a former mountain guide who had become a tea-grower in the Kivu district, and Jean Deru, an agonomist and an excellent climber who also lived in the area. It may be recalled that both men had been my companions on my clandestine visit to Nyiragongo in 1953. With such competent men, I would not have to worry about the security of the men descending into the caldera.

The lava lake, meanwhile, seemed determined to retreat as much as possible. It had continued to sink and was now almost 175 feet below the floor of the caldera's second level; that is, over 1,300 feet below the rim. It had retained its crescent shape but the surface was smaller and the third level was visible, as well as a narrow peninsula on the southern side. This peninsula was the flat inland that we had noticed the preceding year when the level of the lake was low.

The steady shrinking of the lava lake's size over the twelve-year period that I had been observing it was concomitant with its sinking. I interpreted that observation as an argument for the hypothesis that the source of the lake was a stream of magma emptying out at the bottom of the caldera. One never knows whether a lake of this kind is deep or shallow. My own belief is that Nyiragongo's lake is not more than a few yards, or perhaps a few dozen yards, in depth, and that only the lake's "plumbing"—that is, the conduit through which it is fed (called a chimney)—links with a reservoir of magma located at a greater depth. The question of the lake's depth is less futile than it may seem. It has some bearing certainly on the still mysterious mechanics of volcanic activity. Moreover, the correct answer would shed some light on the speed with which magma moves through the surrounding rock.

It is also important for its effect on theories of cystallization and classification of rocks, and for a better understanding of how certain mineral lodes are formed.

The trouble is that it is not easy to measure the depth of a lake of molten rock. The use of sound or ultrasonic waves, as used by ships, or of elastic waves like those used in prospecting for oil, might produce excellent results. But Nyiragongo's inaccessibility and isolation, and absence of any immediate economic return, placed such methods beyond our reach. We had to rely on much less direct methods: for example, estimating the depth on the basis of the time necessary for lava, constantly stirred by apparently regular convection currents, to make a complete rotation. That, of course, assumes that we are indeed talking about a complete circle.

A narrow peninsula stretched out at the southern tip of the crescent-shaped lake.

Our Duralumin supports and the rotating arm.

If so, a given mass of lava observed moving across the surface of the lake, and then sinking in a certain spot or along the crater wall, should reappear at the surface after a certain interval. The length of that interval depends on the extent of its subsurface course and on the speed at which the magma moves through the rock—which is certainly less than the speed at which it moves on the surface of the lake. The simplest technique—indeed, the only technique permitted by our finances—was to mark a given mass of lava with some highly visible substance resistant both to corrosion by the acidic gases and to the extreme temperatures. I had brought along some fragments of heat-resistant brick for that purpose.

For that, however, we would have to descend to the edge of the lake which, at present, was over 750 feet below where we were standing. Where we were standing was already 650 feet below the rim of the caldera. I could see no way other than to start all over with the windlass, rebuild the Duralumin frame and the arm, install the winch and the heavy spool of cable, adjust the guys, steady the whole apparatus with heavy rocks, then run a series of preliminary tests—first with an inert weight and then with a human passenger, just as we had done before. Fortunately this time, there were more of us and while some of us attended to the windlass, the others would have time to help the inexperienced descend the wall. Given the size of our party, getting everyone down that wall would require a good deal of time.

There were about twenty of us, including ten scientists. The first ones to reach the floor of the first level set to work immediately. By chance, the weather was not as bad as in 1958, and we lost less time waiting for the fog and smoke to clear or for the drizzle to stop.

Seismology, magnetism, and gravimetry

Daisuke Shimozuru and Edouard Berg arranged their seismographs at four cardinal points on the terrace. They had already installed similar instruments at the rim, and hoped to do likewise on the second level.

Daisuke Shimozuru, our seismologist.

Guy Bonnet, our geomagnetician.

Pierre Wiser, our specialist in gravimetry and photogrammetry.

A gas sampling. The bottle on the ground at left is full.

Opposite: View from the third level.

Pages following:
Exploring the floating island.

After dreaming of it for eleven years, I was standing at the edge of this fabulous lake.

The skin that formed upon cooling was like a satiny, shimmering metal.

During the afternoon, we returned exhausted to our camp at the first level. We had walked for several hours, but that alone would not have been enough to tire us. It was the intense heat and the bad air that had sapped our strength. Upon our return, I decided not to do any more work that day. The heat had had other effects as well. It had softened and melted parts of our thick rubber soles. In fact, I had a hole in one of my shoes. Also, whatever cotton clothing we were wearing (not wool, which is more resistant),

(CONT. ON P. 120)

there are probably as many quakes at between sixty and 300 miles as there are between six and sixty miles, but many of the former are too weak for their tremors to register at the surface and therefore they escape the notice of seismologists.

Volcanic tremors, on the other hand, usually occur relatively near the surface and are comparatively weak. Their proximity to the seismographs at the surface means that the waves all leave their source at the same time, and all reach the seismograph at virtually the same time. It is not possible to differentiate them on the seismogram, and thus it is equally impossible to gather data from them on the density of the rocks that they have passed through or to determine the mechanics of their origin. It is quite difficult even to locate their epicenters, and still more difficult to determine the depth at which they were produced.

Despite these disappointing results, observatories and volcanological services regard the seismograph as the instrument *par excellence* for sounding volcanoes and attempting to predict eruptions. This preference for the seismograph is based on the theory that all volcanic eruptions are preceded by tremors and these tremors are followed by the rise of magma to the earth's surface. In fact, this theory has been verified in practice on only one occasion. That was in 1959 in Hawaii, when Jerry Eaton studied the tremors and ground swellings of Kilauea, and was able to formulate the most impressive volcanological forecast ever made .

Notwithstanding this success, the validity of this method is open to question. There have been uncounted eruptions without any prior increase in ordinary seismic activity. There have been many quakes (including violent ones, like the quakes at Montserrat from 1933 to 1937 and at Soufrière, on Guadaloupe, in 1956) that were not followed by eruptions.

In 1959, I had not yet attained the degree of skepticism that I enjoy today, and I fully believed that the expedition to Nyiragongo, a volcanological "premier," must absolutely include a seismological program. Since there were no volcano seismologists in Europe at that time, we wrote to the most renowed of them, Professor Takeshi Minakami, asking him to lend us one of his disciples for our expedition. He sent us the best of them: Daisuke Shimozuru.

Daisuke's trip to Africa was an adventure in its own right. His plane made a belly-landing at Calcutta. Fortunately, the crew and passengers were able to evacuate the plane before it burst into flames. Our friend was left only what he was wearing: shirt, pants, shoes. When finally he joined

Our seismographic tent.

us at Bukavu, in the Congo, he offered the most profuse apologies. Not only had all his seismographic equipment been lost in the accident, but also the gifts which, in accordance with Japanese etiquette, he was carrying for us. He seemed particularly upset by this breach of traditional courtesy.

Telegrams, scientific solidarity, and air transport were all combined to assemble serviceable (though disparate) seismographic equipment in rather short order, and Daisuke thereafter never lost his imperturbable and smiling air of urbanity. I suspect, however, that he never quite forgave himself for letting our gifts go up in flames.

After many years of study, Daisuke's teacher and friend, Professor Minakami, had been able to distinguish two kinds of volcanic quakes. Type *A* gave readings somewhat comparable to tectonic quakes. Type *A* quakes

Inside an active volcano, at the Equator—and snow!

Opposite, above: The wall of the pit, illuminated by the lava.

Opposite, below: Twenty thousand square meters of molten rock.

On the second level. In the background are the two walls and, to the right, you can see the top of the floating island.

originate two, three, or four miles beneath the surface. Type *B* quakes, however, are very superficial and therefore unreadable. Another Japanese volcanologist had tried to define the characteristics of these microseismic tremors that accompany eruptive activity. It was Daisuke's intention at Nyiragongo to study any sporadic shocks that might take place as well as the microseismic activity, if there was any. Theoretically, there should have been such activity, since the lava was constantly in motion at the bottom of the caldera. He set up a whole network of counters to be able to compare readings of a single tremor taken at various locations.

The geophysicist of our team was Guy Bonnet who was as tall under his prematurely white hair as Daisuke Shimozuru was short under his shining black coiffure. Bonnet had brought along a magnetic scale—which, despite its name, is not used to weigh anything but to measure the magnetic field of rock. This field varies from place to place, and such variations, or anomalies, reflect the irregularites in the mineral composition of the earth's crust. Such anomalies are more pronounced in volcanic areas than elsewhere, both because of the abundance of magnetic minerals in the volcanic rock and because of the greater magnetic activity in the rock when the earth's extreme heat is so close to the surface. When raised to temperatures sufficiently high enough, magnetic rocks lose their magnetism. Therefore, when very hot magma rises from within the earth and reaches the surface, it is likely that the rock through which it travels will reflect a change in magnetism. The ideal, of course, would be to have a permanent magnet record of such changes in temperature because this would contribute to our ability to forecast an eruption. Thus far, no such record is available. Guy Bonnet, therefore, took up and surpassed the work begun in 1958 by his assistant, Edouard Berg, and was putting together a magnetic chart, the iso-anomalistic curves of which resembled the curves of a topographic map. In the course of later expeditions—a year later, or ten years later—new readings would reveal the changes in magnetism that had taken place.

Meanwhile two others, Mathieu and Evrard, using a gravimeter, were busy trying to unravel the variations in gravity. It is known that gravity varies from place to place, particularly because of the presence of masses of underground rocks that vary in density. If, for example, there were a vein of a heavy metal (iron, copper, tin, gold, etc.) under the sand at a given spot, a gravimeter would give a higher reading above that spot than elsewhere. The gravimeter, therefore, is a very handy tool for prospectors.

In volcanology, it can be assumed that the gravimeter would supply data on both the structure of the subsurface and its composition, as well as the movement of magma within the earth. I say , it can be *assumed*. I myself did not believe that that assumption was correct, but I had no definitive arguments to disprove the beliefs of the physicists. And the latter were very eager to get started with their work, which was to include not only Nyiragongo's caldera, but the entire mountain, as well as the neighboring Nyamuragira and the rift valley in which both volcanoes were situated. I did not know, at the time, that this undertaking would use up four-fifths of the limited funds allocated for the expedition. It required two topographers and two geophysicists, who came from Europe, as well as a number of local people. As it turned out, the results of this expensive gravimetric project were devoid of any volcanological interest.

The torrid breath of Nyiragongo

We had decided to descend into the caldera via the south wall. Since the visit last year, huge pieces of the caldera walls had collapsed. The wall we had used last time was consequently less suitable for the descent, and the south wall was now a better choice. It also had the advantage of saving us the trouble of building yet another camp, this time on the other side of the terrace—with all the work and time that that would have meant in hauling equipment, rerouting telephone circuits, and other such complications. Soon, we almost had a village there. We even had real chickens pecking at real grain as they wandered among the huge tents pitched by the soldiers in as unmilitary a manner as possible. There were separate tents for the seismographic equipment, the other instruments and the library, the kitchen, and our supplies. We used another tent as a dining room and office. The remaining six were for sleeping.

Major Tulpin had brought along a cook whose talents contributed enormously to the morale of the expedition. His name was Sweli, and my memory of him is that of a one-eyed, laughing pirate who lacked only a wooden leg to pass himself off as one of Jean Laffite's crew. He had a genius for devising new and ever more succulent ways of preparing goat and chicken.

His aide in the kitchen was a cook of no less ability, a man named Malisele who was on loan to us from Alyette de Munck. I knew Malisele well because we had been on a number of difficult safaris together. He was an extraordinary cook, as well as an inexhaustible marcher and an intrepid worker with the machete. People who spent only one or two days in his company sometimes thought that he was mute. But, since I knew him so well, I was aware that he spoke as many as ten sentences in a single day.

The soldiers were invaluable in setting up the windlass and anchoring it

During the day, the lake's incandescence was veiled by a translucent skin that reflected the sunlight.

firmly, as was our medic who, since as yet no one was either sick or injured, devoted himself to getting me safely down to the lava lake.

I reached the terrace after a descent very much like that of the preceding year, at about two o'clock in the afternoon of August 12, 1959. I had left Buheno seven days earlier on the trip to Nyiragongo. Experience, the increased size of the expedition, and the relatively good weather had enabled us to gain a week over our 1938 schedule.

Within an hour of my arrival at the first level, Tulpin was standing next

The peninsula with its isthmus barely above the lava and the fjord.

to me. The rest of the day was spent getting supplies down to us and pitching our camp. After dark, we ate a hot meal prepared by our two topside chefs and sent down to us by cable. Then we wandered on the edge of the terrace looking down at the lake until almost midnight. It was as incredibly beautiful as ever. I was fascinated by the alien splendor of the surrounding walls in the reddish-purple light emanating from the cauldron below us. That night in the caldera on the terrace above the ruby-lit lake, we were enclosed by the circular walls with their dancing colors and shadows. We were free to luxuriate in the beauty of the lake.

We spent several hours watching the movement of the lava, trying to establish some pattern, some regularity in any changes in intensity and direction. We again found the geyserlike holes exhaling flames in the same place as we saw them in 1958.

The following morning was taken up with the task of getting our supplies and equipment down to our camp in the caldera. When the men at the rim stopped for lunch, Mylord and I took advantage of the break to explore our terrace by the light of day and to discover the easiest routes down to the next level. The peninsula in the lake, which now divided the southern end of the lake and also formed a narrow gulf reminiscent of a Norwegian fjord, was connected to the floor of the third level by a low isthmus. It was so low, in fact, that whenever the level of the lake rose a few feet, it was covered with lava. This was a danger to keep in mind when we decided to go down to the level of the lake.

During the afternoon, Berg and Evrard joined us. The next day, Berg had hardly finished setting up his first seismograph when he almost crushed Evrard with a large rock that he somehow knocked loose. Evrard escaped unharmed by jumping clear when he heard me yell a warning. Fortunately, I had seen the rock as soon as it began to move, and, fortunately, it moved slowly. Berg himself suffered very painful contusions on his foot and the next day we had to send him up to our doctor.

Despite this accident, we felt that the problems presented by Nyiragongo were only minor, and that our goal was within reach.

Under such circumstances, the usual reaction is to go full steam ahead. My own reaction, however, was in line with my usual practice. I had learned from experience that when difficulties seem to fade, people stop being careful, and that is when accidents happen. I had reached the point where instinct warned me to go slowly, where earlier, I would have rushed ahead. That was what happened at the second part of the descent into Nyiragongo. If I had felt any doubt in my mind about being able to reach the shore of the lake, I would certainly have pushed everyone in our party to the maximun to overcome all obstacles. Obstacles attract as well as frighten, and to attack an obstacle as soon as possible mitigates one's uncertainty. But here, since there were no apparent obstacles, I was determined above all to be extremely careful.

In keeping with this determination, we did not simply climb down the eighty or one hundred feet that separated us from the next level. Instead, we used ladders. This time, we had enough of them and we did not limit ourselves to flexible ladders. For the sake of the men carrying our equipment, as well as for security reasons, we had brought rigid sections made of Duralumin. Each of these sections was about six feet long, and they could be bolted one below the other to make a ladder of considerable length. In addition, we made it a rule that no one could go up or down the ladders unless he was connected to a security rope. (No one, in fact, even asked to be dispensed from this requirement.)

We reached the level of the lake without incident. Then we began picking our way through the rubble of enormous rocks lying between the wall and the huge slabs on the floating island, which were lying at an angle of about 30° to the horizontal. We had to use the utmost care in moving because the rocks were often unsteady. They had fallen only within the past few months, or perhaps within the past few weeks, and the normal process of settling and adjusting aided by the volcano's tremors and vibrations, had not yet made them stable. We therefore had to use our hands and our feet to test any rock before we could trust our whole weight to it.

At first glance, it seemed that this rubble was piled only on the old rocks of the floating island. The island itself appeared probably nothing more than the remains of a former upper floor that had collapsed when the column of magma began to sink. But then we discovered that there were empty spaces under the loose rocks. This could have meant that the island itself was being eaten away by the molten lava around it. Advancing carefully through this kind of underbush of rocks, I heard a whistling sound on my left. I worked my way around an enormous polyhedral rock and found the source of the sound. It was a small depression from which a gas was rising—it was very hot gas because the rocks surrounding this depression were glowing red. This was one of our geysers or holes. We had named it "Brasero" (furnace). All around Brasero were salt crystals that precipitated when the hot gas had suddenly cooled upon contact with the

The floating island.

Opposite: We conquer the third descent.

cool air. Brasero comprised a number of jets, or holes through the rubble. Hovering over each of the jets, and barely visible, was a bluish flame. I felt a strange joy at the sight of the flames. I said nothing to the others about my feelings, but I felt it intensely nonetheless. It is true that we had not yet reached the lava lake, but these jets were an emanation from the lake and were not affected either by contact with the air or by cooling. After so many years, and after so much effort of all kinds, I was standing at the first point from which I could take samplings of eruptive gases that were "pure," unaltered. Those were gases that might contain the answers to the why and how of volcanic phenomena.

Folk wisdom has it that where there is smoke, there is fire. One might add that where there are eruptions, there is gas. These gases are essential to achieving an understanding of volcanoes, but the problem is how to take samplings of them. Dormant volcanoes do not supply them, and usually no one can get near enough to a volcano in eruption to take samplings there. What remains are those rare volcanoes in permanent (and therefore moderate) eruption, particularly those with lava lakes like that of Nyiragongo. Tens of thousands of samplings of gas have been taken and analyzed since the celebrated chemist, Sir Humphrey Davy, first determined the composition of the volcanic fumes from Vesuvius 150 years ago. Ninety-nine percent of these analyses, however, involve only a very small amount of truly volcanic gas mixed either with subterranean water or atmospheric air. It is obvious that such analyses are not very useful in shedding light on the mechanics of magma rises and volcanic eruptions.

At the moment that we gathered around the red-hot rocks that surrounded Brasero, there had been only two series of analyses of gas samplings taken at over $1,000°C$ ($1,832°F$). In both instances, the gases were those taken by Jaggar, Shepherd, and Day during their two visits to the permanent lava lake of Kilauea, in Hawaii thirty years earlier. Two series of analyses are not very much—not enough to be able to draw sound conclusions, and not nearly enough to warrant the professional pride of volcanologists. There we were, filling our specially packaged specimen bottles brought from Paris, with gases at a temperature of $1,040°C$ ($1,904°F$). I took great pleasure in taking up the torch lit by our illustrious American predecessors so many years before and so many thousands of miles away. Those few 200 cc bottles of volcanic gas, which I arranged with the greatest care in their special carrying case, were one of the most precious things that I've ever had.

Big mouth

About 500 feet west of Brasero, we reached the goal of this first incursion into Nyiragongo's pit of fire: "Big Mouth," which was the second of the holes or geysers that we had spotted from above. Because we had no point of comparison, it had been impossible for us to estimate its size. As we approached it, however, we saw that our Big Mouth was actually no more than about three feet square, but the speed at which the gases emanated from it, and the roar of the escaping gas, gave it an appearance of life that was even more striking when seen from nearby. The thought that sprang immediately to mind was that this was a mythological dragon, a fire-breathing beast from a fairy tale. The great flame from Big Mouth, shooting out almost horizontally, which we had looked at so long from the upper level, could be seen only at night. In daylight, it was perfectly transparent and therefore invisible. We approached this roaring monster with infinite caution. I had had a dozen years' experience with volcanoes at close quarters, but here in the fire pit of Nyiragongo, I felt like an apprentice. The roar of Big Mouth was enough to impress even those who thought themselves seasoned by experience.

The conditions for taking samples appeared excellent. Our American forerunners, Jaggar, Shepherd, and Day, had distinguished three classes of sampling for volcanic gases: excellent, appropriate, and mediocre. This classification is based on the purity of the gases of which samplings are made. Generally speaking, the closer the sampling point to the lava and the higher the temperature and the pressure, the purer the sample taken because then the risk of gas being mixed with water and air is minimal. Here, we did not measure the pressure, but it was obvious that it was quite high because of the speed at which the gases were emitted. In fact, the gases were coming out at such high pressure that Tulpin, who is certainly above average in strength—had a great deal of trouble holding the sampling-hose in the stream of gas. On the other hand, according to our readings, the temperature at the entry to Big Mouth was 910°C (1,670°F) and from 990°C to 1,020°C (1,782°F to 1,868°F) one yard inside the mouth. I would have liked to take readings deeper, but our pyrometric rods were only two yards long and, even though we were wearing our fire-resistant clothing, we could not get closer than we were to place the rod deeper into the flaming mouth.

The chemist who would later analyze these samplings had given me two

Taking temperatures with the thermocouple.

Opposite: Rocks are heated red-hot by eruptive gases which, when they cool, leave whitish deposits.

Taking gas samplings.

different kinds of sample bottles. They were all glass cylinders about eight inches long and three inches wide. One type had only a small nipple, which was heat-sealed after a vacuum had been established within the bottle. The second type contained air and had two glass spigots at the bottom, both of which were perfectly airtight. Both kinds included bottles containing a chemical reagent that would stabilize the water condensed from the volcanic steam, and bottles without this chemical reagent. There were four bottles to fill at every sampling point.

The sampling technique was quite simple. We held a six-foot steel hose or tube into the stream of gas and, with the help of a short Teflon hose, directed the flow into the bottle through the nipple. For the bottles with spigots, we opened both spigots for a couple of seconds until the air within was expelled and the temperature stablized. Then we closed the spigots and put the bottle into the carrying case. For the vacuum bottles it was a bit more complicated. Having placed the Teflon hose over the nipple, I snapped off the end of the nipple between my thumb and index finger. Immediately, the vacuum sucked in the gases and a whitish fog filled the bottle. The hose was then withdrawn and, in the same fraction of a second, a glass cap, containing airtight sealant, was placed over the nipple. Because of the very high temperatures where we were working, we had to wear our heat-resistant gloves—which, especially at the beginning, made these manipulations rather difficult.

Since then, we have made considerable improvement in our sampling technique but, at that time, we knew of no other methods, and so we used those established by Jaggar over a quarter of a century earlier. What we found to be unsatisfactory about this technique was the uncertainty it created concerning the proportion of water vapor in the bottle, and also the representative nature of the sampling. The components of the sampling could react with one another, transform themselves chemically, or dissolve in the drops of water that condensed on the bottle. The dosage procedure for the water was not infallible either. It was based on the principle of the acetylene lamp: calcium carbide had been placed in the bottle and, when the volcanic gases entered the bottle, the water vapor they contained reacted with the carbide to produce quicklime and acetylene. Dosage of the quicklime would then allow the proportion of water to be deduced. Unfortunately, the reaction was neither complete nor perfect, and the margin of error was too wide for this method to be scientifically indisputable. I was too ignorant at the time to know any better and, when we had closed and packed the last bottle at the end of the afternoon of August 14, 1959, and had begun to pick our way back toward the ladders, I was filled with a sense of extraordinary well-being.

Under the lip of the crater

The next day, following the same route, we crossed the rubble and, in a bit over two hours of cautious progress, having explored the floating island as we passed it—we reached the bottom level. It was only a few feet wide, and I crossed it with deliberate slowness, savoring the pleasure, after eleven years of dreaming, of having reached the shore of this fabulous lake. The unbearable heat, rising like a wall, brought me to a halt one step from the vertical drop into the pit.

The lava lake was no more than ten or twelve feet below where I was. For the first time, I saw up close the cooling skin at its surface. It looked like nothing so much as faintly gleaming, shimmering metal. I discovered later that the shimmering effect was actually a kind of shivering, produced by the escape of innumerable tiny gas bubbles. This rough-grained, supple surface served as the covering for the vermillion and purple lava under-

neath. By now, I had been joined by my two companions, and we stood by the side of the lake, transfixed by the spectacle.

The lake extended to our left, growing wider in the distance, like an estuary. On our right, it narrowed to form the southern horn of the crescent which gave the lake its characteristic shape. This horn had been forked by the apparition of a peninsula some 100 feet long and twenty to thirty feet wide, with an uneven surface perhaps ten or twelve feet high. The only low, nearly horizontal part was the isthmus which connected it to the floor where we were standing.

It was child's play for us to get over to the shore of the lake. When we reached it, we were standing over 1,300 feet below the rim of the caldera, and no more than two feet away from the lake of molten lava.

The southern shore of the peninsula fronted on a tranquil bay of lava that we had just walked around. The northern edge, however, was splattered by drops of molten rock. At the foot of the cliff where the floating island ended, there was a river of fire, about fifty feet wide, flowing rapidly. We had observed it from above and noted that this stream of lava had its source toward the middle of the lake and that the flow gained speed as it approached the edge of the lake. From where we were now standing, the stream took on an almost infernal aspect. As it flowed between its black banks (the lava turned black when it cooled), the river was characterized by increasingly larger and more violent bubbling until, at the end of its bed, it was swallowed up in an incandescent cavern.

It was an unimaginable sight, almost monstrous, like something from an unreal world. Gustave Doré and Edgar Allan Poe together could not have produced a more diabolical ogre's lair than that cave. Its mouth was scarlet, and from its ceiling hung glowing stalactites, some of which were enormous, like the fangs of a fire-breathing monster. The floor of the cave was of molten gold.

Opposite, above: Big Mouth.

Opposite, below: Taking gas samplings at 1,800°F.

Our camp in 1959.

Opposite: Ready for the first descent.

The seismograph is an instrument based on the principle of inertia. It amplifies and registers vibrations or waves during an earthquake or tremor. The study of these waves—their speed, their time lag, and their significance—has made it possible for seismologists to understand the nature of the earth's interior, at least as far as major earthquakes are concerned. A seismograph reveals almost immediately the location of the epicenter (the central location of the earthquake or tremor), and makes it possible to analyze the nature of the earth movement. Larger tremors that result when two of the earth's tectonic plates move in relation to one another, occur at least two or three miles beneath the earth's surface, and often much deeper. Occasionally, they occur at depths of several hundred miles. In fact,

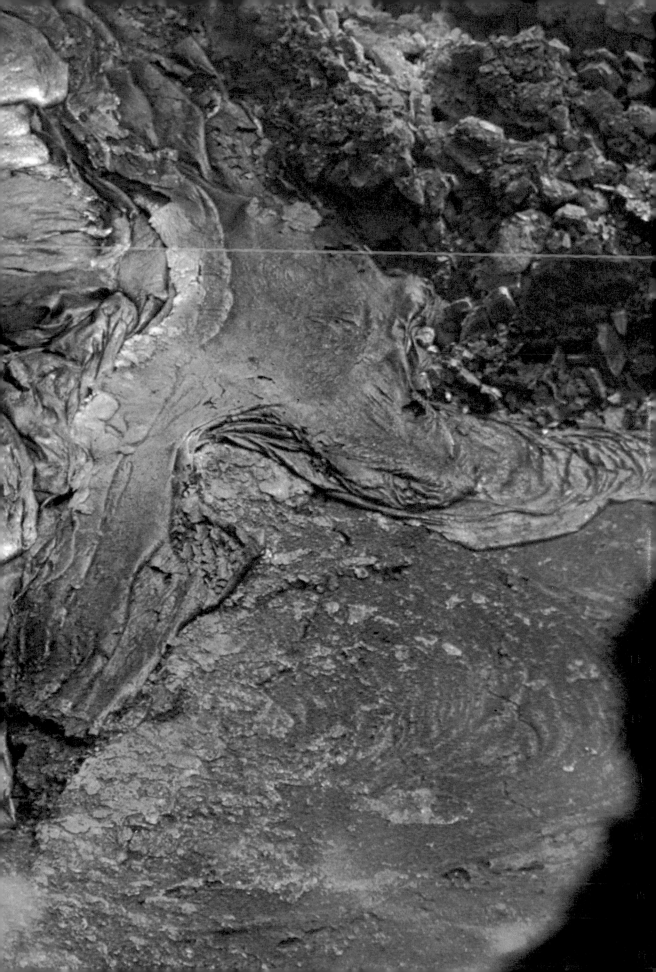

CONT. FROM P.92!

such as our shirts and pants, was hanging in rags, having been eaten by the hot acid gases.

That night, as we lay in our sleeping bags, we all felt absolutely limp from exhaustion, but also incredibly at ease. It's a very strange feeling to reach a goal after pursuing it for so long, with apparently very little chance of ever attaining it. You end up continuing the pursuit, not so much out of conviction as through inertia. At that point, when you attain the goal, astonishment mixes with euphoria and sometimes even dominates it.

Three days of study

The next morning, we sent Evrard back up to the rim and I asked Louis Tormoz and Jean Deru to join us down below. I intended to continue our work of taking samplings and measuring temperatures. The three following days were filled with work. We took gas samplings everywhere possible and relevant to do so: at Big Mouth and at Brasero again, at a vent over which hovered a flame that was apple-green at night, at another vent that gave off orange flames visible only at night, at a crevasse in the floating island. The chemical analyses would show later that the best samplings came from the vents where the pressure (that is, the speed at which the gases were expelled) was highest. Water vapor, when it was able to be measured, constituted between 40 and 45 percent of the total (in weight), and carbonic gas was about the same. Sulfur dioxide was four to five percent; hydrogen, 1.5 percent; and carbon dioxide, two to three percent. The proportion of water vapor in the gas, however, must be accepted with caution. Hydrogen was present in all the bottles filled under good conditions. In the others, it had been burned off by the oxygen in the atmosphere. Compared to the analyses Jaggar had taken at Kilauea, those of Nyiragongo showed a higher content of carbon dioxide and a lesser content of sulphur dioxide.

But, even if these techniques were flawless—which they were far from being—samplings taken in conditions that were hardly comparable cannot be regarded as representative. In order to determine what the exhalation of a volcano really is, it would be necessary to have an extensive series of

We stood on the lowest level more than 1,300 feet below the rim of the caldera.

At the bottom, next to the fjord.

On the lowest terrace, at the level of the lava lake.

The river of lava flowed into an incandescent cavern.

The fjord, seen from the lowest terrace and looking toward the open lake.

Tazieff and Tulpin taking gas samplings on the floating island.

samplings taken under precisely determined conditions of temperature, pressure, and delivery. And, of course, the techniques for gathering those samplings used would have to be beyond question. In order to compare the gases from two different volcanoes, it would be necessary not only to use the same techniques for both volcanoes, but also (if possible) to have these techniques applied by the same people.

During the days and nights we spent in the caldera, we were able to observe that the level of the lake fluctuated by three to fifteen feet, sometimes in a few minutes and sometimes in a twenty-four-hour period. Naturally, we had to be aware of this phenomenon because when the level was high, the molten rock at the surface washed over the isthmus of the peninsula where we were working. It also happened that the lake level would suddenly rise and the lava would quickly overflow part of the ledge at this level. Then it would recede after a few minutes. It goes without saying that, in such cases, we scrambled up the vertical wall without delay, with the lava lapping at our heels like some incredible reptile.

The current that carried the stream of lava from the middle of the lake into the incandescent cavern sometimes reversed itself. I do not mean that the mouth of the cave spewed out what it had swallowed, but that another, weaker current carried lava from in front of the mouth back into the middle of the lake. At such times, it appeared that the center of the lake was lower than the horns of its crescent, whereas usually it appeared slightly higher.

We had to install the seismographs in places that Daisuke Shimozuru indicated. His instructions were both by telephone and in diagrams sent down by the cable. His written instructions were much more helpful than his oral communications, given the different accents of the language we were using (it was supposed to be English). In two weeks, Shimozuru registered fifteen tremors, five of which originated in Nyiragongo. Nine had their source in the rift valley; one was far away. What our seismologist was particularly interested in, however, was microseismic agitation. After a month of study, represented by miles of taped readings, his conclusion was that this kind of agitation, characterized by a time of between one-third and one-half of a second, and by a variation of from 6.5 microns at the base of the caldera to .2 microns at the rim, was caused by the longitudinal vibration of a chimney of viscous magma about 1,650 feet long. The agitation also seemed to have a first cycle of seven minutes, and another cycle of three and one-half days. These complex calculations had

Geysers outside the mouth of the cavern.

Opposite: The fjord and peninsula seen from the second terrace.

The skin covering the lava was hardening into a shell.

convinced Shimozuru that this hypothesis was more probable than that which attributed such microseisms to the slipping or folding of the rock strata that formed the cone of the volcano.

I have mentioned the southern horn of the lava lake several times. The northern horn was equally interesting, even though the activity of the geysers in the lake was much less violent there than in the southern horn. This end of the lake had a cave into which lava flowed most of the time, but this cave did not appear as spectacular as that of the river mentioned previously. The reason may have been simply that there was no equivalent third level on that side from which we could observe the inside.

The current on this side was less swift than on the other side, perhaps because this horn of the crescent, not being divided by a peninsula, was four times wider. On this side of the lake, the lava disappeared into the cave under the overhang. A regular swell, at the rate of six three-foot waves in a ten-second interval, accompanied the current. As soon as the rounded crest of a wave disappeared under the overhang, an explosion from the interior of the cave dissipated it, and the glowing fragments splattered 150 feet onto the supple, steel-colored skin of the lake. These explosions, which occurred at intervals of slightly more than one per second, were quite extraordinary. It's my opinion that they were caused by a compression of the gases within the cave. The arrival of the lava wave brought about this compression, which was followed by a violent combustion of the hydrogen (and perhaps by other components) in the atmosphere. The result was an explosion.

There was a similar swell at the other end of the lake, but it occurred more rarely. However, we did see a truly fantastic sight in the southern horn: waves, fifteen to twenty feet high, following one another at an interval of fifty or sixty feet. It was not only fantastic, it was frightening. And the sense of dread that I experienced while watching that spectacular exhibition was more than the mere natural fear that someone feels when he or she witnesses one of nature's more formidable phenomena. Such displays were rare, and most of the time the lake was relatively calm, except for the geysers at the bottom of the fjord and the activity in the southern horn. Occasionally, even the fjord and the southern horn were quiet, and then the lake seemed to be dormant.

When activity began again, it took diverse forms. Sometimes there would be agitation in the river in the fjord, or the surface skin of the lake would crack and the glowing fissure would spread, spiderlike, over the hardening carapace of the lava. Sometimes, we would see the lava begin to flow in all directions away from a point at the foot of the wall at the end of the floating island, midway between the two horns of the crescent. And sometimes the lava would suddenly swell before our eyes, like dough rising with unrealistic rapidity. The sight of it conveyed a feeling of power, like that of some fearsome animal gifted with unbridled strength.

We took samplings of fresh lava from the fjord every few hours. The current was strong there, and the lava was constantly being renewed. We

The shell of twisted lava.

wanted to know whether or not there was any significant variation in its composition. This kind of sample-taking required a good deal of physical strength. Once the tip of the long rod had been inserted into the viscous magma—which, given the conditions in which we were working, itself demanded a certain amount of effort—the rod had to be manipulated by twisting, very much like twisting spaghetti around a fork. The heat itself was no particular problem, if the person involved in the maneuver was wearing a heat-resistant suit. These suits, although not as impervious to heat as their manufacturer claimed, nonetheless made it possible for the wearer to remain near the heat for several minutes without discomfort. This was more than enough, since it required only ten or twelve seconds to take a sampling. We soon grew tired of putting on the suits and taking them off (which required several minutes of work, and left us out of breath) for such a short operation. Therefore, we soon began wearing only the helmet, which shielded the head and face, and the large asbestos mittens. This protected us from the heat for about twelve seconds—long enough, if we worked quickly. To speed up the process, rather than walk to the sampling point, we started at a run when we were fifteen or twenty feet away, so as to reduce as much as possible the seconds that we had to remain in the heat. With his long arms and legs, with his golden visor down (the special visor-glass was plated with transparent gold), and with his hands clutching the long sampling rod, Mylord looked like Don Quixote as he rushed to attack the enemy.

It was not suprising that even such men as Mylord Tulpin and Louis Tormoz, who were both in prime physical condition, were quickly worn out by this kind of work; one can imagine the effect on the rest of us. Sometimes fatigue overwhelmed us like a great weight pressing down on our backs, and we were frequently tormented by headaches. Nerves, of course, played a part in it, and the nervous strain was as great as the muscular strain.

Our nights in the caldera were often not restful enough to offset the fatigue of the days. Sometimes an unusual phenomenon kept us up most of the night. And sometimes bad weather—rain, dense fog, strong winds, sleet, even snow—made it necessary for us to squeeze into the narrow tent, the canvas of which was being eaten away by the gases. But there were other nights when we fell asleep like kings, under a circular canopy of dark blue velvet sprinkled with stars. I never grew tired of contemplating the night sky lying beyond the rim of the caldera, or the caldera's reddish walls which isolated us from the rest of the world. Concentric, they rose through successive terraces. Above each terrace, there was a dark ring, where the reflected nocturnal glow of the cauldron was interrupted. Each level, in fact, could be identified by its radius, its brightness, and its color. They grew larger and darker; they were colored scarlet, then violet, then purple.

Spectrography

We returned to the rim on August 19. Tulpin and I had been in the caldera for exactly one week. What particularly struck us upon our return was the feeling of safety that we had there. It was only then that I realized the degree of tension and strain that we had endured. This camp was home. It was like returning to civilization. It was a village, with thirteen large tents, three generators, chickens running around, people hurrying about on business, real meals at predictable hours. There was even (because of the military presence) a flagpole and a flag.

After having taken care of several urgent matters, the following afternoon I returned to the camp at the first level to give a hand to our astrophysicist. The previous year, he had been unable to photograph the spectrum of a volcanic flame; this year we had brought back with us a field spectrograph that we thought would do the job.

By then, the old tent was thoroughly eaten away by the acid in the air and had collapsed. We set it up again as best we could, although it was in effect nothing more than a bunch of rags hanging from a wooden frame. Then, until past midnight, we worked to erect another tent to use as a darkroom. When that was done, we set up the spectrograph and focused it on Big Mouth. Then we took pictures, using systematically longer exposure times: three minutes, ten minutes, twenty minutes, a half-hour, an hour. Finally, we developed the film. The results were disappointing. The flame was so slightly luminous that it was barely visible on the prints.

The astrophysicist had a hard time sleeping. He was not used to this kind of strenuous work, and he was literally too exhausted to be able to sleep. He was even too tired to get up and find additional cover to protect himself from the piercing cold.

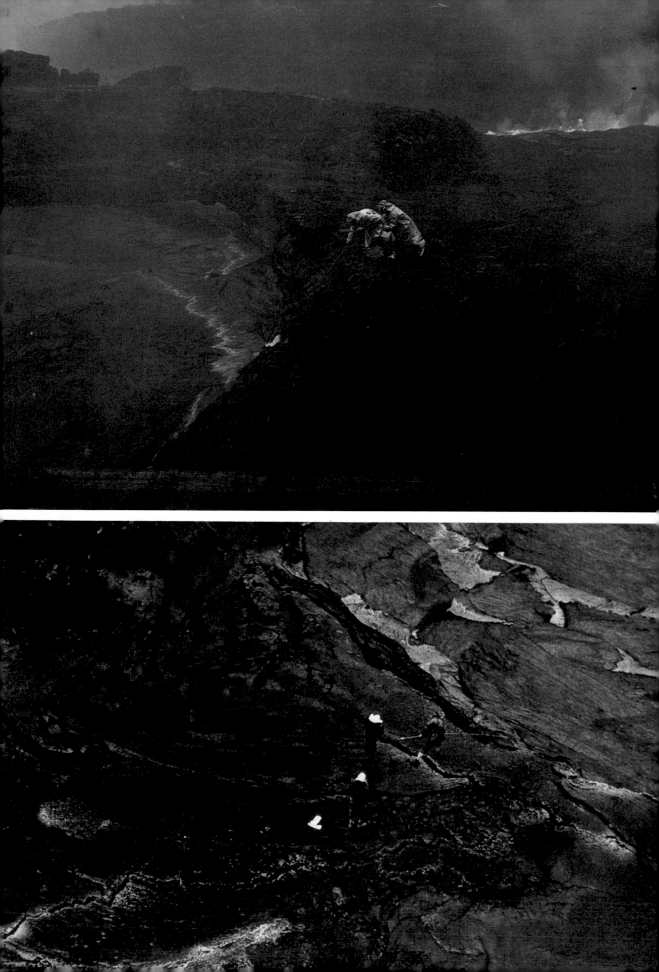

We wore suits of aluminum-coated asbestos and mask.

Opposite, above: To take samplings, we had to stay for ten or twelve seconds in the torrid heat at the edge of the pit.

Below, and opposite below: We took gas samplings wherever it was useful and possible to do so.

The following day, after we had tried to do whatever we could with what remained of our tent, I took him on a tour. We walked around the end of the terrace, looking at the lake. The level of the lava was unusually low, and it occurred to me that, if it went down any further, another terrace would probably be visible. During the three hours of our stroll, we saw the current in the fjord reverse its direction twice. On both occasions, the process began with a reduction in the current speed, followed by a halt in the flow of lava. At the same time, there was violent activity in the geysers a dozen yards from the mouth of the incandescent cave. There seemed to be a strong swell between the area of the geysers and the far end of the fjord. After several minutes, the current began flowing once more, but in the opposite direction. The lava seemed to rise to the surface where the bubbling was taking place and then flow toward the center of the lake at gradually increasing speed. We also noted that the third terrace—that is, the isthmus of the peninsula—for practical purposes, was no longer accessible. I went down lower. The topography of the place had changed considerably in the preceding forty-eight hours. The third terrace had grown, and it now contained an isolated pool of lava.

Night came, and we had to return to the first level and get to work on our spectrographic operations. Except for the current in the fjord (the lava was now flowing once more toward the cave), the surface of the lake was calm. Here and there, we could see apple-green tongues of fire darting over the black surface, between the red and yellow fissures. There were other flames of the same color at the mouths of the caves yawning at both tips of the crescent.

The rest of the night was devoted to photographing the spectrum of Big Mouth's flame. During this ten-hour session, we had ample opportunity to continue observing the lake, its brief furies, its reversals of current, the thick smoke suddenly given off by isolated vents, its period of calm, its overflowings, its accelerations and decelerations, the collapses of the walls of the fjord because of the constant lapping waves of fire, the sudden fall of some stalactite which, overburdened by a build-up of lava, broke loose from the glowing ceiling of the cave.

Finally, the developed film showed the spectrogram of Big Mouth. It was the first spectrum ever obtained of this phenomenon. The analysis revealed, in the visible and near (7,000 to 4,000 angstroms) ultraviolet, a continuum attributable either to calcium oxide, or to nitrogen protoxide, a double line of sodium, a doublet of potassium, and twenty-five molecular bands caused exclusively by the CuCl molecule. The ultraviolet area was entirely without lines or bands. We concluded that the low-energy source of these flames was wholly thermal. With the more or less primitive equipment available, we knew that these were the best results that he could hope for. We spent the next day taking samplings of new incandescent gases and observing the activity of the lake. Then, at night, we took another spectrogram of Big Mouth, with results identical to those of the first.

During the next few days, the other researchers who until then had remained cloistered at the rim, went down into the caldera. Most of them wanted a closer look at the phenomenon they had been observing for the past two weeks from above. But several of them went down with the intention of complementing work they had undertaken higher up. This was particularly true in the case of Guy Bonnet, who had taken a detailed magnetic survey at the rim and now wanted to do the same down in the caldera.

Bonnet was an extraordinary person in many respects. He was by far the tallest member of the expedition, standing over six feet, four inches. He was also consistently the hardest worker. He resolutely ignored whatever pretexts the rest of us found for not crawling out of our sleeping bags (and later, our tents) early in the morning, and he ignored rain and fog to whatever extent it was possible. Anyone courageous enough to rise at the first light of dawn and emerge into the damp cold would see Bonnet's tall silhouette alternately standing erect and hunching over a magnetic scale installed on a tripod. At night, he was the last one to return to camp—and he was not contemplating the lake, but taking a few more magnetic readings. Behind Bonnet's handsome, regular features, there was a raging passion for geophysical research: taking readings, doing calculations at his table. He virtually never spoke. Bonnet was truly a personality.

He took readings at 400 sites in order to measure the magnetic field of the volcano. Moreover, he took over a hundred measurements along a thirty-mile circuit of the slopes of Nyiragongo. The conclusions that he was able to draw from this enormous amount of work were extremely in-

Double page following: The monstrous cave was unimaginable, except in a fantasy world.

teresting for what they seemed to reveal about the structure of the volcano. The interpretation of geophysical measurements, founded as it necessarily is on a series of postulates, cannot be regarded as a certitude but as a hypothesis. It becomes a quasi-certitude only when confirmed by other geophysical or geochemical criteria.

Bonnet had concluded that the interior of the caldera—that is, the successive terraces, the floating island, and the lake—were characterized by a very marked average magnetic inclination of less than thirty degrees, while the volcanic cone had no inclination at all. From that fact, he deduced not only that there were huge pockets of magma beneath the island (as others also believed), but also that the volcano's chimney (the channel through which the magma reaches the lake) could only be narrow.

This was a weighty argument in favor of the hypothesis that the lava lake was shallow and only a few yards deep. It was like a liquid in a plate, entering the plate from a narrow opening in the base, rather than like the upper surface of a column of lava that was almost as broad as the lake itself. According to that theory, the various movements of the lake, such as currents, geysers, and swells, could be explained with respect to the depth of the lake and the width of the chimney that fed the lake.

A formidable power

After three weeks in the caldera, we were exhausted; exhausted, but not idle, because the work of observation and measurement was still going on. Moreover, the spectacle in the caldera could not really exhaust those who appreciated it: the apparent monotony, the constant repetitious bubbling and flowing, moving like the waves of the sea or the current of a river. To this was added the fascination of the unforeseen and the unforeseeable. And, finally, there was the overwhelming impression of formidable power.

This power was visible to the naked eye in the currents that stirred the lava, the bubblings, the waves. The ear heard it in the whistlings and roarings of the gases. And the skin itself felt it in the colossal heat, in the thousands of kilowatts that were radiated and dissipated in the atmosphere without noticeably affecting the humid chill of the upper terraces. The reason for the latter phenomenon was that almost all this heat rose perpendicular to the lake. And, since it rose vertically, it had no perceptible

Our old tent was gradually being eaten away in the acidic atmosphere.

warming effect on the vast circular terrace at the upper level and even less at the rim of the caldera, although the air was no doubt very hot several hundred yards directly above the lava lake.

The astrophysicist, Delsemme, and Bonnet, by methods as different as the two men themselves, each arrived at the same estimate of the energy given off by Nyiragongo: 960 and 930 megawatts for the 13,125 square meters of the lake's surface that year (as computed by our topographer). It is always very satisfying for two independent researchers to obtain the same

Opposite, above: We kept at it, sometimes for ten hours at a stretch.

Opposite, below: The enchanted lake.

An inferno—but a peaceful one.

results, for the results then confirm the validity of the technical approaches used as well as that of the calculations.

So much energy, and all of it wasted. For several years now there have been discussions about the possibility of harnessing and utilizing volcanic energy, especially the energy of volcanoes located in industrialized areas where energy of all kinds is becoming increasingly rare and costly. Certainly it would be technically possible to harness part of that energy, but there would be enormous problems involved. For example, the materials used would have to be alloys capable of resisting the voracious corrosive appetite of gases at a temperature of almost 2,000°F—gases that are a mixture of hydrochloric acid, hydrofluoric acid, and sulfide compounds. Then there is the cost involved in setting up a volcanic energy plant near a like like that of Nyiragongo or on the slopes of a volcano in almost continuous activity. Such costs would be so enormous that no government could possibly accept them, to say nothing of private corporations or international consortiums. Even if it were economically feasible to build such plants, there would still remain two imminent dangers. The volcano might become dormant (in which case the plant would be out of business for years, or even for centuries) or the volcano might erupt and destroy the plant entirely.

Although it seems impractical to harness eruptive energy itself, there is still a fabulous wealth of geothermic energy that is available. I am referring simply to the natural heat that exists in the depths of the earth and that is economically exploitable today wherever winter temperatures require that buildings be heated. This is low-temperature geothermal energy such as geysers where underground water is heated by the earth's internal heat. Volcanic regions, on the other hand, contain high-temperature geothermal energy capable of producing electricity from inexhaustible and nonpolluting sources.

Why has this never been tried before? Because of ignorance, the absence of appropriate technology and, until recently, an abundance of other energy sources. After all, a group of Italian engineers successfully used subterranean steam to power an electric turbine over seventy-five years ago. This occurred at Larderello, in Tuscany; today that same source is still producing three million kilowatt hours per year.

In 1947, while I was still a young engineer working in the Congo, I had the good fortune to assist Anatole Rollet, the director of the tin mine where I was employed, in setting up the electrical system for a vein that we wanted to exploit. At the foot of the hill in which the vein was located, there was a hot spring. Rollet used this source of energy to power a small electric plant; it was the first such plant since that at Larderello. Twelve years later—about three months before the expedition to Nyiragongo—I was invited to visit a new geothermal plant at Wairakei, in New Zealand. I learned a great deal there, and immediately put some of what I learned into practice.

P. B.

Nyiragongo and one of its satellites, Baruta, seen from the north.

4

The misadventures of a volcanologist: 1966, 1967

A benevolent crater   P.B.

The Nyiragongo expedition of 1959 was a success. At least in the sense that we had succeeded in reaching the lava lake, had brought back specimens, had taken samplings of eruptive gases, and had taken a series of seismic, gravimetric, geochemical, magnetic, photogrammetric, and physical measurements which were to be the starting point of a vast program of systematic and coordinated studies. On the other hand, it must be said that these results, because they were not coordinated, of themselves were not all of great significance. It was interesting, certainly, to find out that there was relatively little water in the eruptive gases, that traces of copper had been found in those gases, that the lava lake was probably fed through a narrow chimney, and that the frequency of microseisms might have something to do with the silica content of the magma, but these things were no more than a first step. A promising first step, perhaps, but only a beginning. When I left Nyiragongo, I was already developing that program of studies in my mind, and I was also mentally putting together a competent and cooperative team capable of undertaking those studies. Since we had succeeded in de-mythologizing the descent to the lava lake, it did not seem unrealistic to imagine such a team devoting itself, for years, to the study of Nyiragongo.

Obviously, there were many problems, and some of them appeared insoluble. Nonetheless, I set to work with utmost confidence. Then there occurred an unexpected political development that put an end to my plans. The granting of independence to that vast area formerly known as the Belgian Congo plunged the newborn nation into political upheaval. Civil unrest and famine were endemic; the "authorities" were being overthrown at every turn. It would have been madness to think of taking a team of scientists, with their costly and burdensome instruments, into an area where massacres and widespread unrest were facts of everyday life.

For a long time, therefore, I regarded Nyiragongo as being once more forbidden territory. But, after five or six years, the situation in the Congo (now Zaire) became somewhat stable and my hope was reborn.

On February 13, 1966, at nine o'clock in the morning, I set out from Kibati with Guy Bonnet, his assistant, and a young German seismologist. We had four Banyarwanda bearers with us. By noon, we were at our old camp at Bruyères. The huts of tree trunks and branches had disappeared, no doubt knocked down by storms with the cooperation of the elephants. From that point, it took our bearers one hour to reach the rim of Nyiragongo. For us, it took an hour and a half.

The weather was quite good. There were a few cumulus clouds floating above the banks of Lake Kivu and blocking our view of Goma. There were whitish streaks at a high altitude to the south, but to the north the sky was clear and the two giants of the Virunga range, Karisimbi and Mikeno, were perfectly outlined against a background of blue silk.

Bonnet, who had climbed Nyiragongo only two months earlier, had already told me to what extent the caldera had changed in the six years since I had seen it. Even so, I was astonished. The bottom of the caldera, which had never before been visible from the rim, was now perfectly distinct. The level of the lava lake had risen considerably and was now several dozen yards higher than it had been in 1953 when, so far as we could tell, it had begun to fall and shrink.

An approximate view of Nyiragongo's caldera as seen in clear weather, with no fog, no clouds, and no smoke.

Lake Kivu

To GOMA

KIBATI
(the bearers)

BRUYÈRES CAMP

SHAHERU CRATER
(dormant)

CAMP I

rest stop

supply cable

rubble

descent route

vents

wall

lava
lake

the way
into the pit

P.B

Our descent to the first level took a fair amount of time because an inexperienced member of our party had an attack of vertigo while on the wall. We formed a single line of four climbers and, with each step, we took one of the terrified man's feet and placed it firmly on a foothold in the wall. Thus, it took over five hours for a climb that normally would have taken me between fifteen and twenty minutes.

The second, third, and fourth levels no longer existed. The terraces had all been covered by the lava. The lake was now spread across the entire width of the caldera, an area of about 2,000 feet. The floating island was still there, but smaller, and it no longer backed up against a wall. It was now in the center of the lake. In the sunlight, it appeared light gray. The sunlight itself was a rare phenomenon in the caldera. In the past, it had always been blocked either by bad weather or by gases from the lava. Now I was almost as surprised by the presence of the sun as I was by the changes within the caldera. But the rise of the lake and the disappearance of the lower terraces were not the only changes. Nyiragongo's activity was also different from what it had been. In fact, it seemed to have diminished substantially. The gray lava at the surface of the lake was no longer a plastic skin, but rather a solidified crust or shell that hid the molten rock beneath and the lava's movements. Now there were six small cones in the lake's surface, rising in a semicircle in the eastern half of the lake. The incandescence of these very active and explosive cones could be seen, sometimes even in broad daylight. Their position marked the edge (now covered) of the island. In addition to these miniature volcanoes, the largest of which was about fifty yards in diameter at the base, there were two large vents in the lake's surface, both of which shot out flames. One of these was directly over our former Big Mouth. Despite these changes, there was a surprising air of permanence within the caldera.

We spent the first half of the night observing the volcano's activity, which was much more evident then than during the daylight hours. There were explosions that sometimes sent up red flares to a height of 200 feet and streams of lava that oozed out of fissures in the surface and spread out over the hard shell. We could now see flames at every opening in the surface; sometimes we even saw them spring up over the black shell of the surface. The streams of lava also appeared much more frequent and numerous than during the day, when the light of the sun made them more difficult to distinguish.

I did not know what part these streams of lava played in the rise of the lake since our earlier expedition. The rise in the lake was a result of the rise in the flow of lava out of the chimney, but during the forty-eight hours of our visit, I saw so many of these streams of lava everywhere that I believed they had played a preponderant role. That, along with the large circular overflows that we observed from time to time, would explain the structure of the caldera's walls as innumerable horizontal strata.

The volcano's activity was much noisier and more explosive than formerly. There were more howling "mouths" in the surface, pyroclastic bombs were more frequent and rose higher than they had before, and there were more flames. These phenomena, however, did not necessarily mean that there was more gas escaping than, say, in 1959. The explanation may have had something to do with the existence of the solidified shell covering the lake. Previously the tens of thousands of square yards of lava had no solid cover and gas escaped freely. The lake was now covered by a hardened crust. The gas continued to accumulate beneath this shell, but it could not escape until sufficient pressure had built up for it to break through the crust by means of holes and fissures.

The quantity of energy available, however, had perhaps decreased, or at least had not grown at the same rate as the quantity of magma rising from the depths. The proof of this seemed to me to lie in the very existence of that crust of lava. It had solidified because the amount of heat lost through radiation was greater than the amount of heat now being produced by fresh lava. The lake now had a surface area of about 250,000 square meters; that is, about twenty times what it had been in 1959. It was therefore losing heat through radiation twenty times faster than before. It seemed likely that the flow of lava into the lake through the volcano's chimney, had not kept pace sufficiently to maintain the surface temperature above the point of solidification.

As it was, the volcano offered multiple opportunities for taking samples. There were many vents where the lava poured out in ten different forms: narrow jets, wide bands, rhythmic puffs, continuous streams, violent explosions, and so forth. But in any form, it was always at temperatures of 1,000°C (1,832°F) and over and at pressures clearly higher than that of the atmosphere. Access to these vents, while not easy, was nonetheless possible. I bitterly regretted not having brought equipment to take samplings. Nyiragongo was so benevolent at that time that, even working alone, I could have taken a fair number of samplings. In fact, in 1959 we had left some sampling equipment, carefully greased and packed in wooden boxes, hidden in a break in the wall. But seven years of corrosive gases had taken their toll, and absolutely nothing was usable.

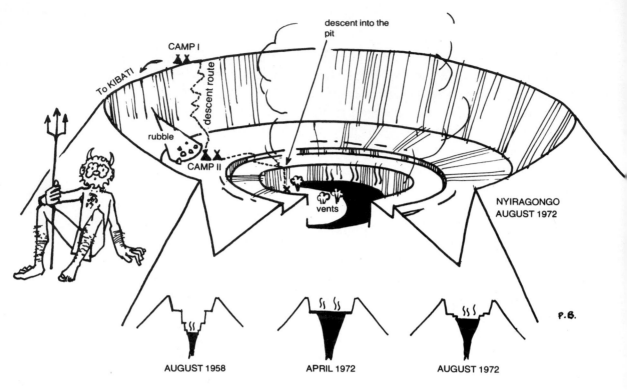

descent into the pit

CAMP I

To KIBATI

descent route

rubble

CAMP II

vents

NYIRAGONGO
AUGUST 1972

P.B.

AUGUST 1958   APRIL 1972   AUGUST 1972

VARIATIONS IN THE LEVEL OF THE LAVA LAKE

A team in mountain climbing shoes and knickers.

As soon as I got back to Paris I set to work organizing an expedition for the following year. Unfortunately, the source of funding that had made it possible to organize expeditions in 1958 and 1959—the Belgian Ministry of Education—had now dried up. Now that the Congo was independent, Belgian funds were no longer available. "Since Belgium has no volcanoes," I was told, "Belgium has no interest in volcanic research."

France, for her part, had not yet taken the step toward volcanology that would have enabled me to set up a major expedition. That step was only a year away, but I did not even suspect that it was so near. Therefore, relying as usual on money from my own pocket, I could only consider an expedition with a minimum number of people and minimal equipment; that is,

The lake was covered, and the floating island had shrunk.

an expedition with a limited goal. I decided to concentrate on taking gas samplings, and I chose two friends, Franco Tonani and Ivan Elskens, both of whom were chemists.

A brief incursion

In May 1967, there was an eruption on the northern flank of Nyamuragira, not far from where the eruption in 1958 had occurred. I took just enough time to pack a bag, assemble a minimum of instruments, and get on a plane for central Africa. I arrived at Nyamuragira on the very day that the short eruption ended. Such are the hazards of volcanology.

I found Guy Bonnet already there, with his assistant and a young geologist named Philippe Guibert. We spent several days at the site, then returned to have a look at Nyiragongo. The closer we came to Nyiragongo, the more interesting this look became. The condition of a volcano at any given moment is so subject to change that the more it can be observed, the better it can be understood. On this occasion, however, I found the volcano little changed from what it had been the preceding year, at least as far as activity was concerned. The surface of the lake was still covered with its crust of hardened lava. The six mini-volcanoes still belched fire from the surface, and streams of lava still oozed from fissures in the crust. On the other hand, the level of the lake had risen noticeably, and the surface now lay at what seemed to be about a hundred yards below the large first terrace. The floating island had also changed, not in shape but in size. It was lower and smaller than before. No doubt this was the result of the accumulation of thousands of streams of lava which raised the level of the lake as well as the gradual erosion of its submerged part by the lava.

Conditions at Nyiragongo were even more favorable than we had thought they would be. The only real obstacle to the rising level of the lake—the height of the interior wall of the caldera—had not only been considerably reduced, but would probably be reduced even further.

Just at that point, a new wave of violence broke out in the Congo. There were battles, massacres, and a reign of terror. The two sons of my friends the Muncks, who were students in Europe, were arrested by the Congolese army when they returned home for vacation. After being questioned at length, they were killed. Then followed the horrors of civil war, and Nyiragongo lost its importance in our eyes.

Mount Etna

In 1968 our present team of researchers in the mechanics of eruption was born*. It had all begun one year earlier, when Georges Jobert, Direc-

*This team was developed by the C.N.R.S., Centre National de la Recherche Scientifique (National Center for Scientific Research), a division of the C.E.A., Commissariat à l'Energie Atomique (French Atomic Energy Commission).

tor of Earth Sciences for the C.N.R.S., was aware of the importance of volcanism and offered me a job as a researcher. I accepted gratefully and immediately instituted a program hinging on the physics and chemistry of gases. But almost at once, I became aware that this program was too ambitious for the financial means placed at my disposal. The C.N.R.S. was unable to increase the amount budgeted for my project, and I therefore began looking around for additional funds. Finally I came across an office of the C.E.A. interested in the undertaking. It was the office having to do with atmospheric pollution. The paradoxical aspect of their interest was only superficial. An understanding of the nature and composition of gases from factory smokestacks or from automobiles requires almost the same techniques as those required for the analysis of volcanic gases. The methods are similar, but not identical, because industrial exhaust is quite differ-

Opposite: There were streams of lava snaking through crevices in the shell.

The covered lake in 1967, and the staircaselike walls of the floating island.

ent from volcanic exhaust. Moreover, the locations where volcanic gases are studied are such that the instruments used must be both independent of electrical sources and light and compact enough to be carried on a bearer's back. Since no such instruments satisfactory in those respects existed at that time, either in industry and commerce or in the volcanological observatories spread throughout the world, it was necessary to begin by inventing, building, and testing these instruments. My new co-workers, Pierre Zettwoog, Camille Vavasseur, Jacques Carbonnelle, and Jo LeBronec, got to work on them, and we selected Mount Etna as our first testing ground.

Etna, like all volcanoes, is quite capricious. It offers great advantages to the volcanologist because it is in a quasi-permanent state of eruption and because it is easily accessible. At the same time, the explosive aspect of its activity makes it somewhat hazardous for a volcanologist working on the edge of its crater. After two years of work, just when we felt we were getting somewhere with our new instruments, Etna lost at the same time both its regularity and its comparatively gentle nature. At that point, I began to think longingly of permanent lakes of lava. I say lakes because in 1967—the same year that we had to give up our new expedition to Nyiragongo—we had had the good fortune to discover another lake of lava: Erta Alè, in the Ethiopian desert. Our 1971 expedition to Erta Alè was very useful, both technically and scientifically. The lava lake of Erta Alè was extraordinarily and even paradoxically tranquil. Located in the middle of the hottest and saltiest desert in the world, this expanse of molten rock looked like nothing so much as a pool in an impressionist painting. This of course made it possible for us to take samplings of gas to our hearts' content—a task further facilitated by the fact that in the preceding twelve years our sampling techniques had improved. I had it in the back of my mind to compare these gases with those of Nyiragongo. When I suggested this to my team, everyone accepted the idea with enthusiasm. I was going to Nyiragongo once more.

Preparations and diplomats

In my absence Nyiragongo had not fallen asleep. Quite the contrary. From time to time, I received news of it from friends living in the area:

Seven years of acidic gases had taken their toll of the carefully greased and packed equipment that we had stored in the caldera.

Alyette de Munck, the geologist Philippe Guibert, and Jacques Durieux, a young chemistry teacher in Goma. I had thought that Nyiragongo was a finished chapter in my life. Instead, I found my interest awakening again. I learned that, since the middle of 1971, the volcano's lava lake was once again free of its crust and the floating island had been covered by the lava and disappeared completely. In the past six months alone, the level of the lake had risen about 150 feet. At that rate, within a few months it would be at the first terrace.

This rise had taken place over a dozen years and was a phenomenon that deserved to be studied. At the same time, the energy produced continued to increase. In fact, the lake now contained between 200,000 and 300,000

On the trail to Nyiragongo.

Opposite, above: Goma and its extinct volcano on the shore of Lake Kivu.

Opposite, below: The level of the lava lake continued to rise.

square meters of lava, each meter radiating 60,000 kilocalories, while during our last expedition there were only about 12,000 kilocalories. Why? How? I wanted to go see for myself and above all take new readings and measurements.

To organize a scientific expedition of ten or twelve people to go to an unpredictable country some 3,000 miles away is not the kind of work that I enjoy. Nonetheless I began with what I had learned from experience was the *sine qua non* of any such undertaking: the diplomatic preparation. I knew of too many missions that had run into problems because they had neglected beforehand to allay any possible hostility on the part of the host country.

I began by requesting the necessary permits from the Bureau of National Parks of Zaire (as the former Belgian Congo was now known). At the same time, I wrote to the government authorities in Kinshasa (formerly Leopoldville), the capital of Zaire, and to the French ambassador in that country.

A quick visit to Kinshasa, in January 1972, made it possible for me to obtain those permits and authorizations that I had, until then, been unable to get either by letter or telephone. I also took advantage of my visit to organize for our future logistical support at Goma.

Nyiragongo was becoming more and more active, and the level of the lava lake was continuing to rise at a rate that I found alarming. It was now only a few yards from the first terrace, and I was beginning to worry that there would be an eruption before August, which was when our expedition was supposed to arrive. If the lava overflowed onto the terrace and continued to rise in the caldera, the pressure exerted on the exterior walls would become dangerous. These walls are composed of varied rocks and are much less solid than those of the interior. Moreover, the wall becomes thinner at the top, and it was not impossible that they would give way under the pressure of the lava. If that happened, the lava—which was exceptionally fluid because of its temperature and its chemical composition—would flow down the exterior slopes toward the surrounding plains at an initial speed that would exceed thirty or thirty-five miles per hour. If the lava broke through on the eastern or southern slopes where there were cultivated and heavily populated areas, it would be a disaster.

I had asked Jacques Durieux, who lived in Goma at the very foot of Nyiragongo, and Philippe Guibert, who visited the volcano more frequently than Bonnet did, to keep me informed of what was happening. If it seemed

The lava was moving with such force that it had jumped large crevasses.

that an eruption was imminent, we would simply have to telescope our projects and preparations and get to Nyiragongo before anything happened. I was worried that the volcano's ever-increasing activity might make it necessary to begin our work before we were thoroughly prepared. And yet at the same time, I was like a child dreaming of a catastrophe. I could not help wishing to see a sea of incandescent lava rising in a volcanic caldera until the pressure of it burst the cone like an overripe tomato.

Meanwhile, I was frantically busy trying to put together a team that would be as complete and as effective as possible. The funds at our disposal were sufficient only to equip and transport a team of four persons. What I had hoped for were four scientists and four climbers. I tried to bargain with various airlines for reduced fares. Initially, they all encouraged me to believe that there was hope, but, one by one, they then expressed their regret at being unable to help me. It was certainly not for lack of effort on our part—not so much my efforts as those of Simone Pepin, my secretary, and of Janine Garineau, secretary at the French embassy in Kinshasa. Without her knowledge of the affairs of Zaire and of how things are done in that country, our expedition may not even have been able to take place.

One of the problems was that it was not nearly as easy to get the necessary permits as I had thought. In Kinshasa, as elsewhere, there were cliques and parties in the upper ranks of the government. In order to get any action on a request, the applicant had to be extremely careful not to step on any toes.

A view of things to come

Despite all our efforts, things seemed to have come to a halt just at the time that Guibert informed me that Nyiragongo's lava lake had overflowed onto the terrace at the highest level of the caldera. Fortunately—or unfortunately, depending on one's point of view—this was an ephemeral phenomenon, and the lake sank back almost immediately. I was very disappointed to learn that there had been no one there to observe the inundation of the upper terrace. Guibert was on Mikeno at the time, and Durieux was sick in bed.

A month earlier, when he returned from a series of visits to the volcano,

Durieux had written to me about the more or less cyclical activity of the volcano over the preceding six months. There were periods of relative calm lasting twenty days at first, then ten days. These periods separated eruptive phases that lasted two or three days, during which the level of the lava lake rose at a much faster rate than at other times. At the end of December, after a rise of over twenty-three feet in a thirty-day period, the lake had nearly reached the first terrace of the caldera. At that point, Nyiragongo lapsed into a tranquil phase, and Durieux did not think it necessary to inform me of that.

Then, during the night of April 7, 1972, the sky suddenly turned to fire. In Goma, which lies at the foot of the mountain only a little more than a mile below the summit, the people were terrified. In Kibati, the villagers were in a panic because of the noise and the tremors. In the camp at Bruyères, a park ranger, hearing the rumblings and feeling the earth shaking, resisted the temptation to climb up to the rim to see what was happening. Instead, he took off down the mountain as fast as his feet could carry him.

The following day, as far as could be seen from a distance of a couple of miles, Nyiragongo was calm again. Bad weather set in, and the volcano was now hidden by clouds and fog. Two weeks later, despite the continuing bad weather, it was possible to get down into the caldera. It turned out that my correspondents had been too hasty in concluding that the lake had overflowed onto the entire terrace. What had happened, in fact, was that great splashes of lava had been thrown upward at high speeds. An indication of their speed was the fact that these jets of lava had jumped over some of the crevices in the floor of the terrace. At the time that it was inspected, the terrace was covered with a two-foot layer of vitreous, wavy, shiny black lava. The level of the lake must have dropped almost immediately, as evidenced by the remains of hardened lava on the terrace. The lake was now a double pit; that is, composed of two stories. It was no doubt the successive collapse of these stories that caused the tremors that had frightened the inhabitants within a thirty mile radius. The tremors were not caused by the eruption itself as some supposed.

The increased activity of the volcano over the preceding year was not in abatement, but could begin again any time and go much further than it already had. It was important that we accelerate our preparations. While I contained my efforts along financial and organizational lines, my teammates worked to perfect the instruments that we planned to take with us. The primary goal of the expedition was to take systematic samplings of

The Nyiragongo caldera in 1972.

Opposite: A twelve-foot wall, instead of a 600-foot cliff, now separated the first and second terraces.

high-temperature gases fusing under high pressure. We also wanted to take temperature readings and, if possible, measure the flow of these gases. It would also be very helpful if we could keep a continuous record of these characteristics as we took our samplings, so that we would know precisely under what conditions the samplings were taken and what the

variations were. For the continual temperature readings, we planned to use an infrared radiometer; for speed measurements, a double correlated telescope. In our laboratory at Saclay, Camille Vavasseur was building the telescope, while Jacques Corbonnelle and Jo Le Bronec were putting the finishing touches on the radiometer. Meanwhile, François LeGuern was preparing our sampling bottles and rods.

I made a second hurried trip to Zaire in June to try to iron out a few organizational problems, to visit the authorities whose cooperation we needed, and to have a quick look at Nyiragongo.

I remained at Nyiragongo for two days—long enough to satisfy myself that, if the volcano's activity remained at its present level, our expedition would be an unqualified success. It is true that conditions were not favorable as they had been six years before. At that time, the lake was covered by the crust of lava, broken only by a few vents and holes which served as escape valves for gases from the lava. Moreover, the gases were under sufficiently high pressure to keep the air from mixing with them until they were expelled from the vents. At that time, the crust was solid enough for us to be able to walk around on it, and it provided relatively easy access to the vents. Now, however, the crust no longer existed. In its place was a tempestuous expanse of molten rock and extremely active "mouths." It would be difficult to reach the latter, but not impossible. At the foot of the vertical 100-foot wall that now separated the terrace from the bottom of the pit, there were some rather wide pathways of solidified rock leading to the various roaring, whistling vents. Also, there was a large panel of rock on the south side of the pit that had been separated from the terrace and was now leaning at an angle of about fifteen degrees, forming a miniature replica of what used to be our floating island. It seemed to me that, if we jumped onto that rock from the terrace, it would not be too difficult to climb down to the hellish-looking lake. Of course, we would have to wear our masks and heat-resistant suits while we were down there. I had already spotted some very promising holes in the lake.

These on-the-spot observations, as encouraging as they were, did nothing to solve my budgetary problems. In fact, once I had seen Nyiragongo's actual state, I was even more worried about money than before because I saw that we would absolutely have to have men who were expert climbers. We needed men with know-how, physical strength, and a dash of *sang froid*, in order to get the researchers to where they were going and to help them carry their equipment. (The most onerous pieces of equipment were the generators.) I had asked several friends, who were expert alpinists, to accompany us. Now I had to figure out a way to pay their travel expenses.

The solution to this problem appeared unexpectedly when one of my American friends, Bill, made two suggestions, both of which I accepted. Bill, an idea man and organizer, proposed to take advantage of the often-expressed desire of young people, especially from well to do families, to get away from city life. That desire, Bill explained, although often tinged with romanticism, led to dreams of taking part in scientific and exploratory expeditions. Bill's idea was to satisfy those longings and, at the same time, to provide both funds and manpower for the expedition.

Bill had set up an organization for such purposes, with his customary flair and efficiency. It was called the Young Explorers, and the purpose of it was to give young people the opportunity to become members of research missions in the field, and thereby to provide the actual researchers with helpers who, if untrained, would at least be enthusiastic. Moreover, the Young Explorers would be a source of funds for the expedition. Bill would be able to get scholarships and fellowships for some of the youngsters, but the others would pay well for the privilege of accompanying the explorers into the field.

The celebrated National Geographic Society, which publishes the magazine of the same name, had expressed a desire to film our volcanological team. The expedition to Nyiragongo, Bill explained, would be a marvelous opportunity for the Society to get some extraordinary footage. We would not be paid anything for our cooperation, but, as Bill pointed out, we would get enormous publicity when the film was shown on television in the United States. This would make it much easier for us to get financing for subsequent expeditions. I accepted, on two conditions. First, the film team was to be limited to three persons; second, the team was to be excluded from the volcano and from the life of our own team. I had already had experience with film people from the French Radio-Television Network on Stromboli and Mount Etna. I had a vivid recollection of a dozen people, three-quarters of them totally useless.

I took comfort in the idea that the money coming in from the Young Explorers would solve many problems on this expedition. And whenever I

Double page following: A vaulted ceiling of moving smoke and light.

thought of the National Geographic Society and television, visions of bright volcanological tomorrows danced in my head. At this point, I should say that those visions never materialized. The Society's film was a great success on television in the United States. We were roundly praised, and just as roundly ignored whenever the question of later financing arose. Even so, my expectations at the time served to free my mind from worry, and it was with utter confidence in the future that I walked into a travel agency and ordered twelve round-trip tickets from Paris to Kinshasa, and that I made arrangements to pay for our several tons of freight. By then I had given up all hope of getting any kind of reduced rate from the airlines I had contacted, and I was resigned to paying the small fortune that was required to transport ourselves and our equipment.

On the day before we were supposed to leave, there was a telephone call from Kinshasa, following which I promptly cancelled the tickets I had ordered. (Since that time, relations between me and the travel agency have been less than cordial.) My secretary took the call, and when she handed me the receiver she was stuttering so badly that I could understand nothing of what she was saying except that Janine Garineau was on the line. I began to stutter too when I heard what Janine had to say. After Janine's umpteenth call to Air-Zaire, the airline finally consented, not to a reduced rate for the expedition, but to absolutely free transportation for all of us and for our tons of baggage and equipment. What was required from me, in exchange, was my signature on a publicity contract in good and due form. Public relations had come to the rescue of scientific research. Anyone who has the responsibility for finding money to pay bills will understand the intense relief I felt at this turn in events.

Somehow—probably through supernatural means—Janine had also arranged for the first class seats aboard the DC-8, en route from Brussels to Kinshasa via Paris, to accommodate all twelve members of our party. As it turned out, however, there were only ten of us. At the last moment, I received a telegram from Moscow, explaining that the two Soviet volcanologists who were supposed to accompany us were withdrawing. They had been unable to obtain official authorization from their government for the trip, even though I had been promised such authorization by the Soviet Academy of Sciences. I was disappointed both because the two Russian scientists were young, pleasant colleagues and because volcanology, which in its modern form is a very young science, can develop only by exchanges at the international level. There are so few qualified volcanologists throughout the world, and so many areas to be investigated, that no mere national team can hope to do everything that must be done. In this case, there was a real community of interests between the Soviets and ourselves in the study of Nyiragongo.

When we arrived in the capital of Zaire, the military aircraft that was supposed to take us to Goma, 1,300 miles to the east, was not there. We waited for an entire week. Every day, new promises were made by the government. And every day, there was no plane. The delay could have been disastrous; I had only enough money to pay for two nights at a hotel for our party, which then had grown to eighteen people. (It goes without saying that hotel rates in Kinshasa were exorbitant.) But, once again, the gods smiled on us. Janine immediately found us rooms in the neighborhood of the French embassy, including some in the same building in which she lived. And I had the honor of being the house guest of the ambassador.

We found Bill and his group in Kinshasa's largest hotel. I was stunned. There were no less than thirty people. And, even worse, they seemed more a troupe of tourists on a guided tour than a group of dynamic youngsters eager to take part in scientific research in difficult terrain. There were even a couple of grandmothers and grandfathers among them, whose presence remains a mystery to me to this day.

Our friendship was to suffer a severe blow in the course of the forthcoming adventure. It began in Kinshasa, as soon as I caught my first glimpse of the mob of Young Explorers participants, chaperones, agents, and organizers. The second blow came a few moments later, when Bill asked that I "give a talk" to his Young Explorers. It appeared that they were growing bored with the hotel's swimming pool, bars, restaurants, and shops. I found it hard to understand how anyone can be bored on a first visit to central Africa, in one of the most beautiful countries in the world, in the middle of a fascinating city, on the banks of a gorgeous river.

We were joined in Kinshasa by the six bearers for our team. They were Laurent and Jean-Luc, aged twenty and twenty-one respectively, who were sons of my old friend, Pierre Bichet. Pierre, in addition to being a painter, was the *sirdar* of our team; that is, he was the boss of our group of bearers. Jean-Luc and Laurent were already experienced hands, having

Double page following: June 1972: At the edge of the pit.

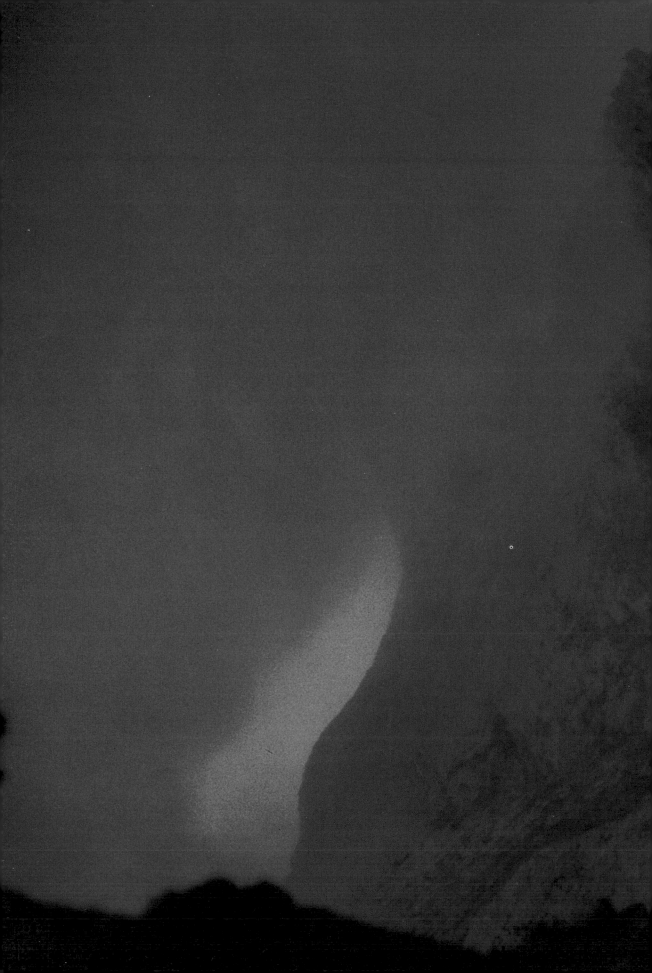

been with us on Stromboli and Etna. They had come by air, at reduced student fares, with two friends: Bernard Griffon and Jacky Grasset. Bernard and Jacky were both bearded and looked like benevolent bears, but bears, I was assured, who were also experienced mountain climbers. The other two bearers were Michel and Yvette Vaucher—both Swiss alpinists of international standing. Michel, in addition to being a mountain guide, is a professor of mathematics; Yvette, since the couple's assault of Mt. Everest, has been known as "the tallest woman in the world." The Vauchers were my insurance that we would have maximum security in our innumerable climbs up and down the walls of Nyiragongo's caldera. Moreover, they were perfect companions for an expedition. It is not enough to be a brilliant scientist or an expert mountaineer to be right for an expedition like ours. A man or woman has to have that nebulous ensemble of qualities that goes to make up what is known as "team spirit."

Goma, beautiful Lake Kiva, the almost animal serenity of the bush, and the use of Alyette de Munck's house as a base, all filled me with the joy of being and of doing. The organization of our supplies and the recruiting of bearers was no problem at all because our friends had done everything for us before we arrived. The two days we spent with Alyette restored our morale, which had been dampened somewhat by the atmosphere, climactic and human, in the capital, and by our limited contacts with our apprentice volcanologists from America. Between checking our instruments, which had fortunately not been damaged in transit, swimming in the lake, and glorious bull sessions at night, time passed very quickly. Finally, on August 2, we were ready to start. Two hundred Banyarwanda bearers, two dozen Europeans, and over two dozen Americans set out from Kibati in small groups and took the narrow trail leading across the savannah and the jungle, with its tangles of vines and its giant lobelias, to the summit of Nyiragongo 5,000 feet above.

Two hundred and fifty people, fifty of whom were supposed to go down into the caldera. It was absolute madness, but I had no one but myself to blame. First of all, I told myself, I had no business organizing an expedition that cost more money than I had. And secondly, I must have been out of my mind to accept blindly everything that I was told about easy money and "free manpower." The fact was that relations between ourselves and the Americans were very strained.

Our caravan spread out very quickly. Before the day was over, it stretched along the entire length of the trail, with the first Banyarwandas putting down their loads at the summit to the Explorers trailing through the jungle and slipping on the muddy path.

Elisabeth Zurcher, who was responsible for keeping fifty people reasonably well fed.

The excellence of our logistical organization almost made us forget the troubles and worries caused by the Explorers. All the material was carried up to the top of the volcano in the first two days, but the food, water, and charcoal (used for cooking) had to be brought up on a daily basis. It required a great deal of experience, patience, and time to organize the operation properly.

Fifty-nine men in a crater

The descent route we used was the same as in 1953. Despite the number of times that we had used it in the past, there were still a large number of unsteady rocks. Now the danger was increased because of the large number of neophytes with us. Fortunately, I knew I could count on a number of experienced people. There was Michel Vaucher, who was a professional; Yvette Vaucher, who was beyond categories; and a group of thoroughly experienced amateurs such as Kurt Stauffer, the third Swiss of our team, an unruffled, peaceful type who was one of our most faithful

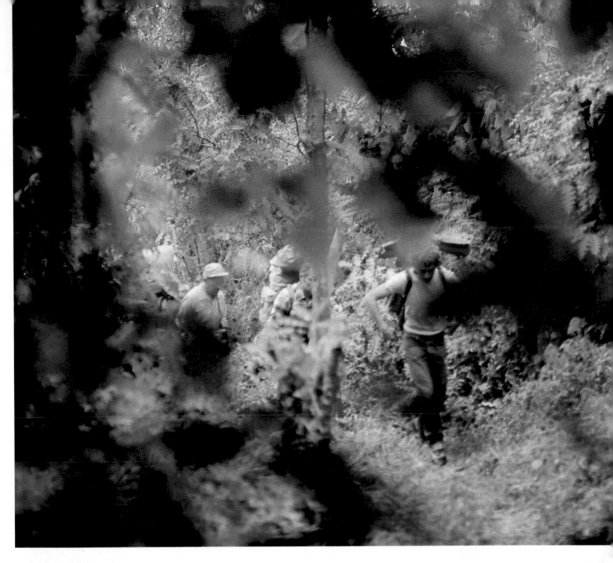

Our caravan set out.

Opposite: Nyiragongo, seen from Bobandana on Lake Kivu.

The Bruyères camp.

Kurt Stauffer and Laurent Bichet.

Above, right: Yvette Vaucher: "the tallest woman in the world."

Opposite, above: Michel Vaucher and Kurt Stauffer preparing the wall for the descent.

Opposite, below: François LeGuern and Michel Loye.

Below: Pierre Bichet, foreman, painter, and chef.

To the left of the lake, there was an incandescent vent in the solid surface about fifteen feet wide.

Opposite: Along the upper wall.

To the left is the large north pool; to the right, the smaller south pool. Between the two is the broken surface of solidified lava.

bearers; Francois LeGuern; the two Bichet boys and their two friends; Pierre Bichet; Michel Loye, Daniel Cavillon—all of whom were putting aside their ordinary tasks to convoy their inexperienced companions down the wall or to transport material down to the terrace.

Our alpinists began by constructing a kind of continuous ramp down the route of descent. It was made of ropes attached to iron spikes which had been driven into crevices in the rock. Then they installed a rigid Duralumin ladder against the only vertical stretch of rock on the route in order to facilitate passage. It took two days for this phase of the work. But, while we were working, we carried down to the terrace what we needed for our camp: mattresses, tents, sleeping bags, and a small supply of food. We were in a hurry to begin getting people down to the terrace because there were now so many people at the rim that space was at a minimum and overcrowding was rapidly becoming a problem. It did not help that there was a strong wind, a disagreeable chill, and penetrating humidity. Also, international relations were not exactly flourishing.

I should have mentioned earlier that, in addition to the seventeen members of our team, the twenty-six Young Explorers, the three members of the National Geographic camera team, and our three local friends, there were a number of other people with us. There was Tom Huntingdon, a young English chemist who specialized in eruptive gases and who had accompanied us to Etna; two English geologists; Thure Sahama, an internationally renowned Finnish mineralogist and an old Nyiragongo hand; a Belgian chemist, Francis Leroy; a French television team comprising three people (who refused to work with the American team); and Christian Vioujard, the photographer. A total of fifty-nine people. The camp at Nyiragongo's rim was as large as space allowed, and it was still much too small for so many people. It had not been comfortable in the best of circumstances; now, it was intolerable. It was urgent to get some of the people out of the camp and down into the caldera.

The volcano's activity had not changed in the past three months. The level of the lake had receded to about 160 feet below the edge, and the large panel of rock that had replaced our old floating island was no longer accessible, since it was now thirty or thirty-five feet away from the terrace. The lava at the surface was now confined to two pools, one to the south and the other to the north. The south pool covered an area of approximately 5,000 square meters; the north pool, about 30,000. Except for the pools, the surface was a mass of black solidified lava, broken only by rises and by a half-dozen vents emitting gases. Some of the vents gave off gas in a steady stream; some, in puffs; and others used a kind of exhaling action.

We would have to use speleological ladders for a span of about 150 feet—which, at an altitude of 11,000 feet is hard work. Other than that, however, there seemed to be few problems. The solid surface of the lake would be easy to move around on, and we would have no difficulty in reaching the vents. We therefore had every hope of being able to get some samplings of rare quality. We would have to be careful of the thick smoke in the caldera. In places where cold and intense heat exist side by side, the wind is often unpredictable, and it sometimes blew concentrated volcanic fumes to unexpected places in the caldera. We would obviously have to use either our gas masks or an independent breathing apparatus. Such were the conclusions we reached on our first visit to the edge of the pit.

The large pool overflows.

Opposite: A vent spews out gas on the shore of the pool.

Eighteen men against a volcano: 1972

The overflow

The first night, there were only a few of us who stayed in the caldera. Only two tents had been erected, and there was very little food and water. After dark, the Vauchers and I stood at the edge of the pit watching the activity in the southern pool of the lake. The other pool was hidden behind a curtain of swirling smoke. There was an equal volume of smoke from the southern pool, but the capricious wind blew it against the wall, away from where we were standing, thereby providing us with a vision of Dante's In-

Double page following: Clouds of steam swirled above the churning surface of golds, vermillions, and purples, taking on the colors of those incandescent waves and swells.

ferno. Above the turbulent surface of golds, vermillions, and purples, the smoke, rising in endless parallel columns along the wall, took on the hues of those incandescent waves and swells. As the columns ascended, they thickened until they covered the sky, forming a fantastically lighted vaulted ceiling over our volcanic world.

This unleashing of the elements, this turmoil of noise and light, was as hypnotic as it was extraordinary. Only our duties, and our fatigue, could tear us from it. It was particularly beautiful that first night because we had been spared the usual blanket of fog. We had been strolling around the terrace, staring at this spectacular example of nature's theatre-in-the-round from every possible vantage point, when we noticed that the large south pool was rising rapidly. In fact, by the time we noticed it, it was already higher than we had seen it until then. It spread over a 1,000-foot crescent the convex edge of which was lapping at the foot of the high north wall, while the concave side was bordered by a vertical wall of only a few yards, which separated it from the stretch of basalt in the center of the caldera. The mass of molten lava in this gigantic cistern was boiling up from depths that varied by as much as ten or twenty feet, sometimes so slowly that the motion of the lava was almost imperceptible, and at other times with surprising speed. Strangely enough, I was more impressed by the slow, placid rise in the level of the pool than I was by the sound and fury that accompanied it. There was an inexorable power about it that struck me as more formidable than the volcanic lightning and thunder at the surface.

As we watched, the pool began rising at increased speed, until it had spread past its hitherto maximum extent. The rise halted for a moment, then began again, only to stop once more. The lava withdrew a bit, but, a few seconds later, began rising anew and continued until it flowed beyond the point that it had attained a few minutes before. The process was repeated a dozen times, with the level of the pool rising higher at each successive stage, until the lava was only a few feet away from the lowest wall.

"It's going to overflow," Yvette said.

It seemed likely that it would, unless the process came to halt. But it did not, and, a few minutes later, the lake was level with the terrace. There, it paused for a moment, almost as though it were hesitating. Then it overflowed and spread out in a stream ten times wider than any I had ever seen before. As we watched in utter fascination, an edge of lava a thousand feet wide spread over an expanse that, seen from above, appeared to be horizontal. The molten rock moved sinuously, silently but swiftly, as though it was starved for space. A smaller stream of molten rock grew out of the main mass and flowed quickly ahead, where it spread into a large semi-circle, like a monstrous flattened bouquet.

I do not remember precisely what I felt at that moment. All I recall is that the three of us turned, ran across the lower footway, and climbed the twelve-foot wall to the terrace. We stopped only when we had reached the terrace, where we stood, gasping for breath, still touched with fear but already feeling slightly ashamed of ourselves. The same thought occurred to all of us: even if the lava continued rising at the same rate—or even if it increased its speed—it would take several hours before it could cover the huge central pit. It had taken ten minutes for the lava to overflow its bed. Before that, its level had had to rise at least thirty feet. A rapid calculation told us that, at that rate of flow, it would take at least two hundred minutes—over three hours—for the lava to fill the five million cubic meters of the pit. But we had panicked before reason could intervene.

We strode back to the edge of the pit, each of us determined to show not the slightest hesitation. By then, the overflow had halted. It was as though nothing had happened. There was the pool, in its usual place, bubbling away, its surface several yards below the top of its cistern. There were, however, long red lines zigzagging across the black rock which had not been there before. As the new lava cooled, its hardening skin shrank and broke, exposing the red lava beneath. The preceding night, there had been a sudden intensification in the volcano's glow, and I had quickly dressed and hurried to the rim. Looking down, I saw nothing unusual except some red zigzag lines between the two pools.

"Ah," I had lectured myself, "there's something I hadn't noticed before. Cracks in the surface of the lake. The crust is not nearly as thick as I thought. We're going to have to be extremely careful when we try to walk on it." What I had seen, obviously, were not cracks in the surface itself, but tears in the cooling lava of an overflow. And the sudden increase in the

Double page following: The cauldron of bubbling lava.

brightness of the volcano's glow had been caused by the overflow itself, which had subsided by the time that I reached the edge of the crater.

Yvette, Michel, and I sat at the edge of the pit, watching the pool and catching our breath. After three days of constant work, our mad race at an altitude of 11,000 feet had left us exhausted. How good it felt to sit still and let ourselves be mesmerized by the hypnotic movement of the lava.

As I looked, a new worry took shape and substance in my mind. I had, of course, not discounted the possibility of an overflow like that which we had just witnessed. To be sure, it was nothing more than a minor inundation, but, even so, a question nagged at me. Should we take the risk of going down into the pit? Ten or twelve minutes had elapsed between the time that the lake began to rise and the time that it began to overflow. Was that long enough to allow a team at the bottom of the pit to get back to the terrace? I saw the whole thing again: the rise of the lava broken by brief periods of subsidence, the apparent hesitation of the glowing lava when it reached the top of its bed of black rock, the overflowing along the whole length of the pool, the silent and rapid flow of the broad river of lava.

Now that we had gotten over our fright, we were totally absorbed by the spectacle as it varied according to the topography of the lake's rocky superstructure. The lava on the part of the lake furthest from us was spreading smoothly and evenly. But on the part nearest us, some very unexpected things were taking place. The most advanced stream of lava was approaching the most violently active of the mouths in the surface, and we waited with bated breath to see what would happen when the two met.

The main body of the moving lava, meanwhile, reached a low wall in the surface—which we had been unable to make out from above—and diverted the torrent, sending it against a column of black rock which divided it into two streams. The larger of the two flowed into a dark canyon, illuminating its walls and making it easy for us to follow the lava's course at the bottom of the canyon. The other stream, on the left side of the column, reached a pit in the surface and, from there, poured like a burning waterfall into the pit, which was several yards deep. Then, as we watched, the pit filled and the lava overflowed, streaming toward the right and finally uniting with the larger stream once more.

At that moment, the most forward stream of lava reached the vent which was shooting out blue flames which, because of the intense pressure, rose to a height of about a hundred feet. As the stream of lava divided and began to move around the vent, part of the molten rock began pouring into the yawning mouth and, an instant later, the transparent blue flames from the vent were embellished with hundreds of thousands of golden sparklike drops of lava. I wondered if the lava would simply flow into and be absorbed by the lake underneath, or if it would smother the vent. It was a struggle between two relatively unknown forces, and it fascinated us. The more lava flowed into the vent, the more dense were the drops of lava in the vent's flaming gas. Soon the flow of gas was interrupted by what seemed to be a gigantic cough. This was followed by the violent expulsion of an enormous volume of red, incandescent mucus. The force of these gases was such that, for a moment, it halted the influx of the molten lava. But then the inexorable flow continued undisturbed. The tide of battle had turned.

Second by second, the rate at which the gases were expelled was diminishing, and the roaring of the gases became less intense. There were now moments of silence, followed by coughs which, while still violent, were noticeably weaker. The vent was being smothered. The process of extinction was punctuated by deep rumblings and occasional coughs, but these became fewer and fewer. Finally, there was nothing left but the tentacles of the lava flow, like a fire-breathing octopus, moving across the surface where the vent had been, silent, indifferent to the fate of the extinguished vent.

Gradually, as the river of lava continued its progress, the remainder of the noisy vents suffered the same fate and the volcano, little by little, became silent. Finally, the only sound was the muffled rumbling rising from the waves, swells, and bubblings of the pools. The whistling and howling and paroxysmal roars, always startling and sometimes silent in their intensity, were now stilled. Until then, I had not realized how much of the noise in the caldera came from the vents. Now that they were silent, the rumbling and splashing of the pools was like silence to our ears.

Except for a few black rocks, protruding like bleak islands in a sea of red, the entire bottom of the caldera had been covered by the overflow. The smoke from the smaller lake to the south had now vanished, and we could see that this lake, too, had overflowed and mixed its lava with that from the other side of the crater.

Everything was now calm, almost peaceful. Almost without our noticing it, the drama came to an end. Suddenly, the flow of lava ceased. I turned toward the north lake and saw that its level was now several yards lower

An arm of lava hurried forward of the main body, spreading out into a large semicircle and looking for all the world like a monstrous, flattened bouquet.

Opposite, above: The cooling skin cracked, revealing for a moment the flaming lava underneath.

Camping on the banks of the lake.

than the huge rocky superstructure in the center of the pit. Within a few seconds, the entire surface, except for the lakes themselves, lost its glow as a black crust formed over the molten rock. Large volumes of lava began to flow back toward the descending lakes, tearing this crust and revealing once more the incandescent lava underneath. Then, the incandescence dimmed as the surface cooled once more, and finally disappeared again beneath the new crust. Soon, the first vent belched, and began spewing out gas. Then another, and another. Once more, the air was filled with whistling and roaring and rumbling. Life in the volcano was back to normal. From beginning to end, the entire drama had not lasted fifteen minutes.

"Well. . ." Yvette murmured.

She had summed up our state of mind accurately. What, indeed, could we have said beyond that? We looked at one another, smiling vaguely, knowing that we were still somewhat in a state of shock, and realizing that our fatigue was not the sole cause of it.

Farewell to the Explorers

We crawled into our sleeping bags and the three of us, all squeezed into the tiny blue tent, slept like rocks. We were ravenous when we awoke at dawn and, since there was no food or water in our embryonic camp, we quickly scrambled up to the rim of the caldera and into the main camp in search of breakfast.

Eating and drinking—especially drinking—is of great importance on volcanological expeditions. It is not that the time of the meals, or the meals themselves, for that matter, are of special interest. It is because the time we spend on and in volcanoes is a period of very intense work. There is the physical work—climbing, carrying equipment and supplies, etc.—and also the mental work and intellectual concentration required by our research. In addition, an active volcano does not have the most relaxing environment that one could ask for; there is a certain amount of constant nervous strain. This means that we absolutely require a certain minimum number of calories every day. Moreover, the quality of food plays an important part in the morale of volcanological expeditions, and morale is something that the head of an expedition must always be very concerned about. That was the main reason (other than considerations of friendship) why we had a painter as a member of our expedition. He was not there to paint landscapes, but to boost our morale by his humor, his happy disposition, and his ability as cook. Pierre Bichet's work was cut out for him because the situation that prevailed in the topside camp was far from pleasant. Everyone suffered from it: scientists, film teams, Explorers. Only our sherpas, or bearers, were kept busy carrying equipment and acting as guides and seemed to be content. To them, life was hard but beautiful.

During breakfast, I broke the bad news to my fellow team members. Since the rises in the lake could not be foreseen, it was impossible for us to remain in the caldera. This meant that we would have to give up our project of taking samplings of the high-temperature and high-pressure gases. The danger was simply too great. The lava spread out so quickly that it might be impossible for anyone to escape in time. Or, at least as we decided after much discussion, the danger was too great to warrant the risk involved. It was a very painful decision. It was all the more so because we were not at Etna or Stromboli, which are easily accessible, but in central Africa, involved in a distant and costly expedition. However, we had to be guided by reason. I have a great deal of admiration for Captain Robert Scott and his companions, who died of exhaustion on the trek back to their camp from the South Pole. But my model is Ernest Shackleton rather than Scott. Shackleton tried to reach the South Pole four years before Scott's expedition. He came to within forty miles of his goal—and then turned back because he had not enough food with him to cover the rest of the distance and still return to camp. That, to my mind, took real courage. He was only six days' march away from the Pole—at the end of an expedition that had begun sixteen months earlier, and after traveling over 700 miles by sled in seventy days. Because of that heroic decision, he was able to get his entire party back alive. At a much more modest level, I've given up more than one summit, and a number of craters that would have given us much data. On that basis, therefore, we decided that we would have to confine ourselves to projects that could be carried out from the terrace of the caldera.

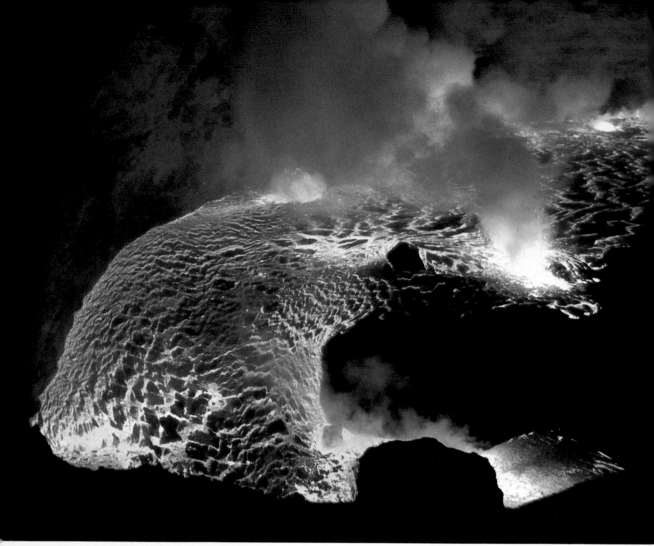

Over the vents, there was a haunting ballet of tentacles.

Opposite, above: The glowing torrent of lava swirled around a pillar of black rock.

Opposite, below: The incandescent surface began to cool and harden.

We still had to get all of our equipment and our people down to the terrace, and we got to work on this immediately. Part of our team worked inexhaustibly getting equipment from the rim of the caldera down to the terrace, while others were busy shepherding the neophytes down the slope. We had to stagger the descents so that rocks knocked loose by a party high on the wall would not fall on a party below. I had issued stern orders absolutely forbidding anyone (except experienced climbers, of course) to attempt the descent without an accompanying guide.

Urged on by the impatience of his charges, the next day Bill put together a descent group of six persons—which was too many—and started down the wall. As soon as we had begun to take groups down, I insisted that some of the Explorers be included among the "elect" who were leaving the narrow and windy confines of the camp for the comparatively spacious terrace. Thus, Bill had made several trips up and down the wall, showing a certain natural ability as a climber. Unfortunately, he now felt too sure of himself, which is a dangerous sign. Only two weeks before our arrival at Nyiragongo, a high school teacher had lost his grip when he reached the first vertical drop on the wall and plunged five hundred feet to the bottom of the crater. He was killed instantly. Sure enough, Bill's group had no sooner started down the wall than there was a near accident. Kurt Stauffer, who was going down carrying a heavy load of equipment, was hit by a rock knocked loose. The rock struck Stauffer, dislocating his shoulder. Only Kurt's skill as a climber made it possible for him to maintain his hold despite the impact of the rock and the pain, and even to complete his descent. It was really nothing short of a miracle that he was not killed. Poor Bill acknowledged his responsibility for the incident, apologized profusely and vowed that nothing like it would ever happen again.

We spent several days in our descent operations, during which time we set up a camp on the terrace. It was adequate, if not particularly comfortable. We also ran a steel cable from the rim of the caldera to the terrace,

Opposite, above: At our camp on the crest of Nyiragongo.

Opposite, below: From left to right: Yvette Vaucher, Laurent Bichet, Pierre Bichet, and Jacques Carbonnelle.

A bag of food is lowered by cable from the rim down to the camp.

Opposite: The upper wall, half covered by streams of solidified lava variegated in whites and reds.

which we intended to use for ferrying food and equipment. As soon as the radiometer had been tested, Jacques Carbonnelle and Jo LeBronec set themselves up on the edge of the pit and began measuring the flow of heat given off by the lake. The radiometer was set at an angle of three milliradians which, at that distance, represented a diameter of thirty centimeters (a little under twelve inches) at the surface of the lake. The gray-black skin of the lake, the red lava, and the fountains of boiling gold could thus be studied at leisure, either by focusing the apparatus on one area and measuring the flow as the various kinds of surface were carried into range by the action of the lake's current, or by focusing the radiometer successively on various places of interest. The median flow, as it turned out, was twice as high as that which Guy Bonnet had measured with his bolometer in 1959.

Pierre Zettwoog and Camille Vavasseur, however, encountered technical difficulties with the double-telescope radiometer that they had built to take long-range readings of the speed of gases and of variations in temperature and concentration. Part of the radiometer was not getting electric current from the battery, and despite the continued efforts of the two men, they finally had to give up. The prototype of the instrument had been tested successfully two months earlier on Stromboli. And the day before starting up Nyiragongo, the radiometer had been working when we tested it again at Aylette de Munck's house. Obviously something had happened to the instrument while being transported—either that, or else the humidity and the corrosive gases of Nyiragongo had gotten the better of it. The fragility of their instruments is a problem that volcanologists have still to overcome. Such instruments must be sturdy, but they must also be light—which is almost a contradiction in terms. And they must be light, as well as complex, which is just as contradictory. Yet, sturdiness, lightness, and complexity are all equally indispensable qualities of a volcanologist's tools. They must be sturdy because of the way that equipment is transported; that is, on a carrier's back, which is not the gentlest way of being carried. They must be complex because complexity, instead of decreasing, necessarily increases to keep pace with the need for precise, continuous, multiple recorded measurements—which are the only hope of ever understanding eruptive phenomena. But, as everyone knows, the more complex a machine is, the greater the chances that it will not work at any given moment. This was the case with Zettwoog's and Vavasseur's radiometer. It was another hard blow to our program.

Since it was now out of the question for us to go down to the bottom of the caldera, we decided to study Nyiragongo's smoke from the edge of the pit, where the smoke passed as it rose upward. These fumes rose rapidly along the south wall which dominated the convexity of the lake. They swelled into enormous gray-white clouds, and poured out of the caldera to form the smoke that, in clear weather, was visible from a considerable distance. Obviously, by the time we were able to take readings, these gases were no longer virgin. The air and the humidity had already altered their

Yvette and Michel Vaucher during one of their countless treks up and down the interior wall. We finally gave them the collective nickname of Yo-Yo.

P.B

Carbonnelle and LeBronec checking out the radiometer.

Opposite, above: The infrared radiometer.

Opposite, below: Pierre Zettwoog and his double correlated telescope.

composition in the fifty yards that separated our vantage point from their source in the lake. Even so, these gases were far superior in quality, and more rich in data, than the vast majority of such gases studied anywhere else in the world. Moreover, they were the only gases accessible to us. We would have to have been very selective indeed to turn up our noses at them. Except for the gases studied at Kilauea by American volcanologists, at Surtsey in Iceland by Sigvaldasson—and by ourselves at Nyiragongo in 1959 and, later, at Stromboli, Etna, and Erta Alè—no one else had ever had access to emanations as close to their original state.

Despite the fifty yards that the gas had to travel before it reached us, and

the consequent cooling because of expansion, it was still burning hot when it reached us (between 250°C and 170°C, or 300°F and 340°F), and still concentrated enough to asphyxiate us. We had to wear heat-resistant clothing and gas masks. François Leguern and Jacques Carbonnelle set up sampling hoses at the edge of the pit, with the "uphill" ends of the hoses held as far down as possible into the thick clouds of gas swirling upward along the wall. The fact that the small tips of the tubes were lower than the downhill tips is part and parcel of the paradoxical world of volcanic eruptions, in which fluids sometimes behave in apparent contradiction to the laws of nature. Gases rise upward, except for pure carbon dioxide which, at an equal temperature, is heavier than air and may flow downhill on slopes. Lava, however, does not always run downhill in slopes. Sometimes—depending on its viscosity—it builds uphill.

Jacques and François set up their collections of sample bottles (the shape and nature of which varied according to their intended uses) at the downhill end of the sampling hoses. Along with the bottles, they also installed their equipment for obtaining direct readings of the percentages of certain components, their filters for gathering salts formed when the temperature of gases fell, their impulse-counter for measuring variations in radioactivity, and, finally, their apparatus for the continuous measurement of sulfurous gases which Jo LeBronec installed about twenty feet from the edge of the pit. LeBronec and I spent the next few hours crouched next to this instrument, operating it and filling our notebooks with the figures gathered by our two friends kneeling at the edge of the pit in their shining metal armor. This was another aspect of the paradoxical nature of volcanology: on the one hand, there is the unbridled and crude power of the phenomenon being observed; on the other, the fragility and complexity of the volcanologist's instrumentation. We were dressed in astronaut's uniforms because of the swirling clouds of sulfurous gases, the showers of hot ash, and the whirlwinds of black sand generated by differences in temperature. These sand whirlwinds raised painful blisters on every square inch of unprotected skin. Fortunately, there was very little skin not covered by the

Opposite: The swirling clouds of smoke rose up the wall next to the lake.

aluminized heat-resistant suit and the asbestos gloves. In fact, the gloves got quite a workout.

One of our problems was fatigue, which was beginning to be chronic. Work of all kinds kept us on our feet from dawn to night. Some people spent their time climbing up and down the wall almost continuously, ferrying equipment to and fro. For the rest, there was scientific work, which was equally exhausting both physically and mentally. The bad weather was such that it was impossible to rest unless we used a tent, and the tents had been designed only to accommodate sleepers. They were too small just for relaxation. In addition, during the first four or five days in the caldera, our supply lines left much to be desired. There was one twenty-four-hour period in which the only drinking water we had was rain water gathered from hollows in the rock. Except for some who feared hunger and discomfort less than they did climbing up and down the wall, those working in the caldera climbed up to the camp on the rim at night. Pierre Bichet gave them a warm welcome and a bottle or two of red wine to take the edge off their fatigue before serving up some sumptuous stew. What Bichet could not understand was why the supplies for the party in the caldera were not reaching us. Some of the Explorers, it seems, were eating the food and drinking the water set aside for returning workers from the caldera. We had so little water that we did not feel that we could even wash our hands and faces. I decided immediately to get all of the Explorers down into the caldera for one final visit, and then to ask them to leave immediately for the plains at Rwindi, which was a tourist's paradise. We did relent sufficiently to grant a dispensation to four who were noticeably more curious, energetic, and enthusiastic than the others.

In the meantime, the camera team from the National Geographic Society had fully integrated into our team and were pleasant companions and did their work with a high degree of professionalism.

Frights and fears

There were several occasions during the first half of our stay in the caldera when we were frightened; even a few when we really experienced

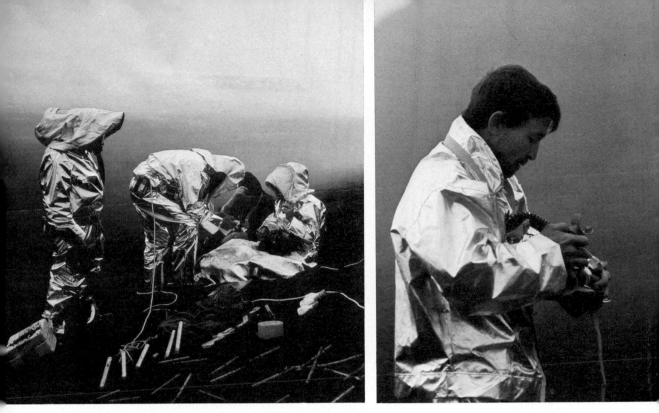

Left: Back from the edge of the pit, Jo installs the SO₂ analyser.

Right: LeBronec in his armor.

fear. There was one night in particular when Nyiragongo's roarings and rumblings began to increase in intensity until the noise was almost unbearable. There was a drizzle falling, and we were all so exhausted that we didn't even have the strength to crawl out of our sleeping bags and look down into the pit to see what was happening. Finally, the continuing escalation of the noise and our ignorance of its cause, combined with our state of complete exhaustion, had its effect. Some of our party hurriedly put on their boots and began climbing up the wall to the rim—illuminated by a purple glow from below—to the camp where, if quarters were more crowded, they were at least relatively safe from the fury of Nyiragongo. The action was contagious, and soon there were only three or four of us left in the camp on the terrace. Camille Vavasseur remained there because he mistrusted his climbing skills even more than he did the volcano's noise. Yvette Vaucher remained because fear of any kind is foreign to her nature. Kurt Stauffer was there, simply because he is Kurt. And I was

Newly solidified lava.

there because I had just gone to bed and I was too tired and lazy to get up again. Also, I was already hardened to the noise of volcanoes, and I figured that the uproar was probably due to an increase in the rate at which gas was being expelled through the vents. That increase was very likely the result of a slight rise in the level of the lake. I didn't think that this justified abandoning the heavenly warmth of my sleeping bag and my cozy tent to go running out into the cold and damp.

A challenge

I think it was just about that time that I became aware of something that served to reawaken hope in me. I had never seen the lake of lava overflow

Among the tuffs of the upper wall.

except at night. I asked the others about it. No one could recall ever seeing an overflow during the day. At dusk and dawn, yes; during the night, yes. But during the day, never. On the other hand, we could all recall no less than ten such overflows during the night. There seemed to be no explanation for this phenomenon, but there was also no doubt about it. It may have been coincidence, or it may have been the result of some chain of causality of which we were unaware. All I knew was that the result itself interested me. If, in the days to come, that rhythm was maintained and daytime tranquility continued to alternate with nocturnal overflows, it would become possible to consider a descent into the pit for the purpose of taking a small number of readings and samplings. I had hope once more.

My companions were not of the same opinion. Pierre Zettwoog, with all the rational thinking of a graduate of the Institut Polytechnique and despite almost four years spent around volcanoes in the somewhat relaxed company of naturalists, did not think the project worthwhile, particularly in view of the risks involved. In any case, he pointed out, it would not be possible to stay down long enough, and in sufficient numbers, to do justice to the job. He was certainly not in error in that respect. But Zettwoog did not seem to be spurred on, as some people are, by the challenge involved in this undertaking. Even François LeGuern, who I was certain would be on my side, declared himself to be resolutely opposed to the scheme. I understood later that his decision had more to do with his state of exhaustion than with Zettwoog's intellectual arguments. He was thin, always working—climbing, running, observing, making notes, playing the accordion, cooking, discussing, demonstrating the Tyrolean art of yodeling. He was literally living off nervous energy. It did not help much that we ate so poorly and irregularly, alternating periods of famine with belt-busting extravaganzas. Camille Vavasseur, for his part, was neutral. The key to his character is gentleness combined with rigor, benevolence with lucidity. Of my five teammates, there were two who never, under any circumstances, ever raised their voices. One was Zettwoog, and the other was Vavasseur. And, heaven knows, volcanology is an occupation in which there are many opportunities to raise one's voice. So, while LeGuern, Carbonnelle, and LeBronec regarded volcanoes with an affection in which romance and a taste for sport mingled with scientific interest, and while Zettwoog looked down somewhat on anything less than scientific and confined himself to problems of thermodynamics and fluid mechanics (in which volcanoes abound), Vavasseur, a gentle, soft-voiced and smiling engineer, felt out of place in the harsh, alien, mineral universe of Nyiragongo. When we had all gone down into the crater to watch the eruptive phenomena which so fascinated us, Vavasseur was the first to see a tiny oasis of grass and modest yellow flowers at the foot of the wall which somehow had survived the immense inundation that had covered the upper terrace on April 7th. He had been absolutely enchanted by this discovery, and it had colored his relationship with Nyiragongo much more than the inorganic might of the volcano.

Jo LeBronec, a sinewy bundle of muscles and nerves, I suspected of concealing (out of respect for Zettwoog, his supervisor) a heartfelt desire to go down into the pit. Jacques Carbonnelle, a massive, flexible man of sometimes surprising urbanity, seemed to take neither one side nor the other, although his character was such as to push him forward rather than hold him back in an undertaking of this kind.

Without arriving at a decision one way or the other, we went back down to the terrace to continue the operations at hand. The weather was improving not at all. Fatigue was gradually decreasing our effectiveness. Nonetheless, our general situation was much more pleasant now that there were comparatively few of us left, the three French television cameramen and their three American counterparts having all left by then. Our food supply was now excellent. The supply of wine, however, was exhausted.

I was now spending more and more time observing variations in the activity of Nyiragongo. And I was becoming more and more tenacious, despite the reticence of my friends, that we should try a descent into the pit. The day went by without a single overflow, the first one taking place shortly after five o'clock in the afternoon. The streams of lava on that occasion covered only the northern half of the superstructure of the lake, but a half hour later, there was an inundation that covered absolutely everything. There were three more before we went to sleep, and another one before dawn. Then there were no more overflows until the following evening. (I mention these overflows just in passing. Actually, they were every bit as impressive as the first one that we had witnessed at such length.) I tried to think of reasons why the lake should be calm during the day and so active at night, but no plausible explanations came to mind. At first, it occurred to me that the rise and fall of the lava might be something like the ebb and flow of the tides of the sea. But neither the duration of the rise and fall of the lava (approximately eleven hours for each), nor the position of the moon supported this hypothesis. Moreover, if it really was a question of some kind of terrestrial tide, why were there level-changes of short duration during a single night? I had to concede that the explanation of the phenomenon probably lay not up in the sky, but in the core of the earth. If so, the fact that the activity occurred only at night seemed coincidental. And, since it seemed coincidental, would the apparent regularity of the lake's rise and fall continue long enough for us to risk going down to the bottom of the pit?

Double page following: The glow from the lava lake at dusk.

There was no way to answer that question. Instead of trying, I decided to accept the volcano's challenge—on one condition: if another day and night passed without any variation in Nyiragongo's schedule, we would try to go down the following day late in the morning. I said "late in the morning" because that would give us another half-day to test the lake.

I noticed a certain coolness when I communicated this decision to the scientists of our team. As the head of the expedition, the research program, and the team, I should have tried to dissipate that coolness. I did not do so, and that was a mistake on my part. The fact was that exhaustion, which weighed as heavily on me as it did on the others, disposed me more to irritation with my companions than to discussion with them. I was irritated that, instead of expressing their disagreement openly and thereby starting a debate on the question, they shut themselves up behind a wall of silent disapproval; that is, silent in my presence, but quite articulate when I was not there. What they disapproved of, I think, was not so much the risks involved in the descent, but my motives in wanting to undertake it. They were quite right in thinking that those motives were not purely scientific. It is true that the real scientific importance of a descent would be reduced to a minimum by the impossibility of staying down long enough, of having a sufficient number of researchers with me, and of risking too much of our equipment in this adventure. If I was so bound and determined to go, they believed, it was for two nonscientific reasons: first, because I could not resist the sporting challenge, and second, because I wanted the film, which we had been shooting since we left Kibati, to have the psychological impact provided only by the sight of men in direct confrontation with nature. Pierre Zettwoog totally condemned the idea of any sort of challenge, and he would admit the artistic validity of a descent into the pit only if it were completely subordinated to the goal of scientific research—which, in this case, was not so.

All of the scientists, in fact, were more or less uneasy over the importance accorded to the television film. Not only were there four cameramen and two soundmen, as well as a French producer and an American producer, but, during the first few days in Nyiragongo, the volcanologists had thought it very unpleasant to have to go without food and water "for television." This complaint vanished once our supplies of food and water began to reach us intact—and especially once we found out that our honest and hardworking television crews had had nothing to do with the disappearance of our supplies. At this point, however, their innocence did not matter. After ten days of incessant work and cumulative fatigue, everyone was convinced once more that a television film was an impure motive for doing anything. But no one was willing to discuss that conviction openly. Perhaps it was out of respect for the "old man" (me); perhaps because it would have been hard to make a rational defense of this position in an open discussion; or perhaps because they had simply had their fill of fatigue, dirt, discomfort, Nyiragongo, and me. That night, everyone went back to Pierce Bichet's camp. The next day, they would take infrared radiometer readings from the crater's rim, which, given the three milliradians of solid angle at which the instrument was set, would allow for the integrated measurement of flow in a circle of almost two square meters.

There were a half-dozen overflows during the night. The spectacle varied according to the vantage point from which it was observed. The best view by far was from the southeast. It was the most formidable torrent of lava that I've seen in more than a quarter of a century. It poured out of the smaller (southern) lake down a steep slope ending at a fortresslike formation of rock the outlines of which appeared only as a dark silhouette against the red lava. It turned out to be the enormous panel of rock which, at the beginning of the year, had been detached from the wall of the terrace where our camp was, and which had been moving further and further away from the wall as it disintegrated into several colossal blocks. Into what bottomless gulf was that river of molten rock pouring as it moved at between thirty and thirty-five miles an hour? There was no way of knowing. We stood petrified as we watched the torrent of fire, stirred by violent bubblings and, at times, rising in great waves, as it rushed behind that fantastic fortress to be swallowed in an abyss that we could not see.

I was up at dawn, and I found that Nyiragongo had resumed its daytime tranquility. The two lakes were back in their respective beds, bubbling and lapping away, while the vents in the lake's crust of rock rumbled and whistled and gave off their transparent flames. The day was spent in getting equipment back up to the rim from the terrace: generators, instruments, samplings of all kinds, and as much as we could spare of our camping equipment. When darkness came, the caldera once more was illuminated by the fairy lights of successive overflows.

The next morning everything was in order. It was understood that, if there was no overflow in the forenoon, we would try to go down into pit. I used the walkie-talkie to tell Bichet what we were going to do, so that he could notify anyone topside who might be interested. It was not until then that I learned that Zettwoog and Vavasseur had left.

"Left? Where have they gone?"

"Left," Bichet repeated. "Gone. They had as much of Nyiragongo as they could stand."

When I saw Vavasseur later in Paris, he explained that he and Zettwoog had felt so dirty, so tired, so irritated by certain aspects of the adventure, that they could not stand it another minute. And since the scientific work was finished, they had decided to return to Goma.

H-hour

For the first time since we reached Nyiragongo the weather was good. A circle of clear sky served as a roof to our cylindrical world and, beginning at eight o'clock in the morning, we were bathed in a solar warmth the pleasure of which we had almost forgotten. Carbonnelle and LeBronec were the only ones working on the rim that morning, and they were busily measuring the flow of heat with their infrared radiometer. Daniel Cavillon, Michel Loye, and the American cinematographers were taking advantage of the weather to get some film footage. From time to time, we looked down at the lake to make certain that it was not rising. The unexpected good weather, the unaccustomed amount of light, the fact that we had finished our program of research, and especially the fact that there was only a dozen of us left in the vast circle of the caldera—it all made us feel like schoolboys on the eve of summer vacation.

Michel and Yvette Vaucher undertook to climb Nyiragongo's "grand dike," which is a vertical intrusion, or column, of lava that has solidified. It ran the entire length of the wall. At the level of the terrace, it is about eighteen feet wide, and from that point it becomes progressively more narrow and finally disappears completely about 650 feet above the terrace. The dike has a whitish patina, which is the result of the oxydation of the magma that formed the column. The rock is a form of leucite nephelinite so rare that it attracted our friend Thure Sahama from far-off Finland. The same grayish-white color also characterizes the old solidified magma streams, or sills, which lay between the layers of rock in the wall. They are distinguishable from the strata of reddish tuff, which are composed of small pebbles, sand, and ashes thrown off by explosive eruptions. The volcanic cone itself is composed of alternate strata (sometimes regular, sometimes irregular) of tuffs and sills. The collapse of the Nyiragongo peak, by which the caldera was formed, had exposed the wall in such way as to reveal part of these strata, thus making it easy to determine the composition of the volcano's interior wall. But, in addition to these horizontal strata, the wall also contained a series of light-colored veins of solidified rock which intersected the wall at angles of up to ninety degrees. These veins or dikes are actually faults, or cracks—now filled with solidified rock— through which lava once spilled out onto the exterior slopes at a time when the large caldera of today did not exist. At that period, not only was Nyiragongo much higher than it is now, but the magma was much higher in the chimney through which the lake is fed. When a break appeared in the side of the cone, either because of increased pressure or because of some subterranean tremor, the lava spilled out through the crack and spread onto the exterior slope. Then, when the eruption was over, the streams of lava hardened on the surface, thereby building up its height somewhat. The magma that was still in the faults also hardened, but more slowly because it was shielded from the cold air. Volcanologists call these veins *dikes*—a term that, in geology, is used to designate the volcanic material filling a vertical fissure or crack in older rock.

Nyiragongo's grand dike is the only one that runs up the entire length of the wall. It is also the most elegant climbing route in the caldera. In 1959, unable to resist the temptation, I had climbed about one-third of its height. Then I beat a prudent retreat. I was aware of the risk that a solitary climber runs—a risk that, in my case, was aggravated by the fact that, in 1950, I had seriously injured my foot. Since then, I had pretty much given up climbing. When Michel and Yvette began their climb, everyone gathered on the terrace and on the rim to watch the graceful maneuvering of these two expert alpinists. From beneath, we lost sight of them toward the end of the climb, at a point when they seemed almost to have reached the rim of the caldera. Then we saw them again, two tiny silhouettes against the sunlit sky. It was noon and noon was *H*-hour for our attempt to climb down to the bottom of the pit.

While Yvette and Michel, Daniel Cavillon and Michel Loye (who had filmed the climb from above), François LeGuern and Pierre Bichet all climbed down from the rim by the usual route, we began getting ready for the descent into the pit. First we measured the distance, using a rope weighted with a rock, so as to determine how many ladders we would need. It is an unpleasant feeling to reach the bottom rung of the lowest section of ladder and find yourself still hanging fifteen or twenty feet above where you should be. We calculated that we would need at least 160 feet of ladder to cover the distance. When we had hauled back the rock weight onto the terrace, one of the bearers—and then a second, third, and fourth—gingerly touched the rock with their fingers. They wondered, rather naively, whether it would still be hot from the heat at the bottom of the pit.

It was not too hard to get our line of ladders in place, especially since Kurt Stauffer and the two Bichet boys had already had experience in such projects. As they worked, I worried about Laurent, who was leaning over the edge of the terrace, shaking the ladder to disengage it from some obstacle. I worried about rocks falling on us as we climbed down the ladders. I even worried about the possibility of the pools overflowing while we were at the bottom. I tried to dismiss this particular worry as ridiculous. Even if there were an overflow, which was most unlikely, there was very little chance of any kind of accident unless someone panicked. Still, I could not

help agonizing over the possibility. The most dangerous aspect of the actual descent was a section of fragmented rocks which formed a ledge about sixty-five feet below the edge of the terrace. The ladders hung free until they reached that ledge. Then they leaned against it before once more hanging in the open air from that point to the floor of the pit. It was conceivable, certainly, that once a man had passed that point on his descent, his weight and movement on the lower part of the ladder would knock loose some of the rocks of the ledge. If that happened, the rocks would certainly fall on the climber. Since he would still be on the ladder, there would be no way for him to get out of the way. I concluded that I had better climb down to the ledge first and clear away the loose rocks. I intended, once I had finished clearing the rocks, to go down to the floor of the pit and take samplings from the four vents nearby. I put on my heat-resistant suit, my hard hat, and a pair of heavy leather gloves. I also hooked a sturdy geologist's hammer to my belt. Finally, after I had buckled on my security rope, Laurent adjusted my mask of rubber and glass, checked the tiny electric ventilator that made it possible to breathe effortlessly through the thick filter cartridges, and hooked up the battery that powered the respirator. I was ready.

By then, every worry had vanished. I climbed onto the ladder and started down the wall, spreading my legs as far as possible so as to push myself away from it with my feet until I reached the point at which the ladder hung free. From then on, there would be no problem. All I would have to do would be to climb down, holding the ladder firmly with my hands and making sure that each foot was solidly planted before I put my weight on it.

As soon as I reached the ledge I saw that it was very unstable. No doubt it was being eaten away by the fumes from the lake. Certainly, the lake had reached this level and remained there long enough to erode the wall with its waves and its hot acid exhausts. I set to work, using my boots and my hammer, knocking away great chunks of rock. I was delighted. Every rock and every shower of pebbles that fell now reduced the chance of accidents later on. It was hard work, but not as hard as I had thought it would be. That, of course, meant that the ledge was even more unstable, and therefore more dangerous, than I had believed. It took me five or ten minutes of work to clear away the worst of it. By then, I was sweating profusely inside my metallic suit, and I decided to rest for a moment before attacking the other half of the ledge. Then, suddenly, I could no longer breathe. In the best of circumstances, suffocation is not a pleasant experience. It is particularly unpleasant when you are already out of breath and hanging from a ladder inside a volcano. I hung there for what seemed an eternity, gasping for breath. I had run races in my time, but never in my life had I had so much trouble simply to inhale.

As I struggled to get the necessary minimum of air, I thrust out my arm twice in the signal, well known to speleologists, which means "up." (Once means "stop"; two means "up"; three means "down." It never occurred to my friends above that I was already in trouble. When they saw my signal, they concluded that I had finished cleaning up the ledge and wanted to continue on down to the bottom. So, instead of hauling me up by the security rope, they began to let out more rope. I moved a step closer to panic. There was no way that I could climb up the ladder under my own power. And, instead of pulling me up, my friends were giving me more rope. As I watched the slack in the rope grow into an increasingly long loop, I knew that if I lost consciousness and let go of the ladder, even for a moment, that would be the end. There was no way now that the security rope could even break my fall, let alone keep me from falling.

With one arm I continued signalling frantically: "Up." And, with the other, I clung to the ladder for dear life. It was another eternity, it seemed to me. Actually, it was only a few seconds before my companions understood that the last thing I wanted was to go any further down into the pit. I then started climbing the ladders and, at the top, was hauled up onto the terrace by many pairs of hands. I was so exhausted that I literally could not even raise my hand. Ladder-climbing, even with the help of a safety rope, is hard work even in normal surroundings. At 1,100 feet of altitude, it is debilitating. But to do it wearing a gas mask that makes it almost impossible to breath—that is not my idea of fun.

It took only a minute to find out what was wrong with my mask. Either my hammer or my elbow had brushed against the battery's on-off switch and cut off the current. All I would have had to do was to turn it on again. It goes without saying that we immediately fixed all battery switches to the "on" position with strips of adhesive tape.

We still did not know what it was like down at the bottom of the pit. I was in no condition to have another go at it until I had had a good rest. If I waited until then, it might be too late in the day and the pools might begin to overflow. I still wanted to be the first to reach the bottom, but what if I made everyone wait, and the overflows began ahead of schedule? I decid-

An eagle at dawn.

Opposite: The large dike was the most elegant route of descent.

ed that someone else would have to go. Michel Vaucher began to suit up. I insisted that he go through the arm-signal code several times. ''One: stop. Two: up. Three: down.'' Then he started down the ladder. Fifteen minutes later, he was digging around on the black floor of the pit that had fascinated us so much for the past ten days. We were all delighted, but Michel more than the rest of us. Michel, without removing his safety rope, made a quick tour of the bottom, showing that it was safe for us to undertake a brief scientific survey of it. Actually, it would have been possible for us to do a much more lengthy and ambitious program of samplings and measurements that afternoon, but we were too jittery to do it. We had all been affected to some degree by the pessimism of some of our party. Moreover, we were all working under a heavy burden of fatigue. Michel, in fact, after climbing back up with the help of his rope, was completely exhausted when he reached us. To anyone who knows Michel and his powers of en-

durance, that was a more than sufficient indication of the condition of the rest of the team, and of the hostility of our volcanic milieu.

François LeGuern, who was in charge of the gas samplings, and Kurt Stauffer, the oldest and most experienced of the team, were to go down together and take samplings from the vent closest to the bottom of the ladder, which was about twenty feet to the right. It was not the ideal place for samplings because the flames came from the vent in puffs. Moreover, the vent alternately exhaled and inhaled. In the latter case, it pulled in fatal quantities of air. The samplings, therefore, even at that extraordinary temperature, would necessarily be diluted by oxygen. The largest vent which gave off a continuous jet under high pressure was three times farther away from the ladder (which was the only means of escape in case of an overflow) and it was to the left, which meant that it was much nearer to the pool and to any possible overflow.

Michel Vaucher on the large dike.

Left: Starting down the ladder.

Right: A touch of safety.

Opposite: On the overhang.

Kurt had been getting ready as Michel was climbing back up the ladder, and he lost no time in replacing him on the rungs. He reached the bottom in ten minutes. Meanwhile, up on the terrace, there was a surprise in store for me. François LeGuern, an eternal volunteer for difficult assignments, now refused this particular mission. This was the first time in four years that he had worked inside a volcano, and this was an assignment that really involved very little danger. But he refused it. Now, his habitual good humor was replaced by a sulky stubbornness.

"OK, François," I said. "Are you going to get ready?"

"No!" he answered angrily.

It was not until later that I understood why. It was fatigue, and that insidious lassitude, both physical and emotional, that affected us all to a certain extent. Also, Pierre Zettwoog's justified criticism with respect to the scientific worth of this undertaking had strongly influenced LeGuern, as

witnessed by this extract from his notes: "Tazieff wants to go down to the level of the lake. I won't go. I've thought about it for the past four days, and I've decided not to take the chance. I have no intention of trying to scramble up 125 feet of ladder with hot lava licking at my butt." That was not the LeGuern that I had known such a long time.

"François," I said, "if you don't want to go, I can send someone else. There are a lot of people here who'd jump at the chance. But you're the specialist in gas samplings."

It was true. Laurent and Jean-Luc Bichet, Patrick Allard, and Philippe Guibert all would have liked nothing better than to climb down into the pit. But, as soon as I suggested that one of the Bichet boys might go down, their father almost bit my head off.

"Are you out of your mind?" he screamed. "My boys? Absolutely not! Do you hear? I forbid it!"

He shrieked the last three words with unbelievable vehemence, glaring at me defiantly. Here was a Bichet that I had never seen before.

Fortunately, the quarrel went no further because, at that moment, François decided that he would go down after all. Possibly he did so to avoid trouble between Bichet and myself.

"All right, I'll go," was all he said. There was no smile, and obviously no enthusiasm about going.

So, François was going, but he was obviously going reluctantly. "Keep a good grip on the rope," I told the boys. It was a perfectly useless instruction, and I knew it. François was in no danger of falling, and the boys were in no danger of letting go if he did. But I felt I had to say something.

Fifteen minutes later LeGuern was at the bottom of the pit with Kurt. We let down their equipment on a rope, and they began searching for the best place to take their samplings.

For us the bottom of the pit had changed completely now that there were men on it. It was not so much a psychological change as much as that we now had a frame of reference. The small human figures moving about in their metallic suits among the black rocks and the flaming vents enabled us to get an idea of the size of the latter and also to distinquish certain physical details which, when seen from above, would have passed unnoticed.

The area where they were working was considerably lower than the turreted rock fortress that we had noticed before, and also lower than the central part of the lake's rocky superstructure. During overflows, streams of lava flowed toward that area and the large incandescent crevasse next to which François and Kurt were filling their bottles then formed fabulous cataracts of red lava and viscous black crust.

Despite the high emotions of a while before, a sort of euphoria now took hold of those of us who had remained on the terrace above. A glance at the pool of bubbling lava far to the left, and another at that on the right behind the men, was sufficient to assure us that there was not yet any sign of a rise in the level of the pools. And then our eyes automatically returned to the two men, encased in metal, working nearby. Everyone now felt certain that there was no danger of accidents, and nothing even to worry about. Having been exorcised of the vague fears and almost irrational apprehensions that had gradually beset us in the past ten days, the sight of our two men at the bottom of the pit made us feel that we were once more masters of ourselves and of what was possible and impossible. Now that our little scientific excursion into the pit was actually taking place, we all realized that, if an irrational fear had not prevented us, we could have very easily carried out our original research plan in its entirety: take samplings from the vents, observe the lava pools, record the temperatures and the flow of heat at the vents. Now, it was too late. Some of our team had already left. The instruments were already packed. But, above all, we were no longer sufficiently motivated. We had simply run out of steam. So much the worse for us. It would be a lesson for us, and we could hope to gather, at some point in the future, the precious data that had eluded us during this expedition. Still, such opportunities are rare, and it is a mistake to let one slip by. I had indeed allowed such an opportunity to escape, and already I regretted it bitterly. There are, above all, only two active lava lakes today. One is at Erta Alè, and the other at Nyiragongo. To study either of them, all sorts of permissions and permits are necessary. Unless you have ample means at your disposal, it is necessary to have the active support of the highest government officials, in Ethiopia as well as in Zaire. This involves a long period of preparation, complicated overtures, and much patience. I had always been able to summon up the required degree of patience. Would I be able to do so again?

Will I ever return to Nyiragongo, the volcano that has fascinated me for more than a quarter of a century? I do not know. It is not that Nyiragongo no longer interests me, or that I am afraid of it. It is that there is something grotesque about having to ask for all sorts of permissions in order to do some scientific research on a volcano. No one needs permission to study a

LeGuern and Stauffer at the bottom of the pit.

Opposite: François and Kurt crouching next to the pit and manipulating their sample bottles.

star, or the clouds, or a mountain, or the course of a glacier. Why a volcano?

Meanwhile, the samplings completed, Kurt began climbing up the long string of ladders. François stood below, waiting his turn for the ascent. He was now himself again, delighted at being where no men had ever been before. I could tell because, as I watched, he turned and strode off for a last look at the lake of lava.

Kurt is going to bring up our sections of flexible ladder.

Epilogue

NYIRAGONGO '74

To the bottom of Nyiragongo

I had just finished the final chapter of this book when I ran across Laurent Bichet, Pierre Bichet's eldest son, and his friend Roland Luetey. He had just gotten off a plane from central Africa.

"You haven't heard," he told me, "but we've been down into Nyiragongo. Down to the bottom. Six feet from the lake! And it was easy!" His eyes shone with pleasure. Laurent, at twenty-three, was already an old hand at volcanoes. He had been on our expedition to Nyiragongo in 1968, and he already had six years of experience under his belt. Now, as he told me about his visit to Nyiragongo, there was a softness, almost a tender-

The edge of the central pit in 1974. It has been pushed upward by the rising magma.

In 1974, the large slabs of rock had been broken down and now formed a kind of staircase leading down to the lake.

As soon as the lake became relatively calm, the surface began to cool and was covered with an opaque skin. The incandescent lava underneath is visible through cracks in this skin.

ness, in his voice. Roland, though less loquacious than Laurent, obviously was every bit as enthusiastic as his friend.

"We were really lucky," Laurent told me. "First of all, we were able to get permission to go down into the caldera. They [the Bureau of National Parks] are very strict about that now because there have been so many abuses. Since we were there two years ago, they've installed rungs and permanent ladders on the walls, and hundreds of tourists were going down. Jacques Durieux took down dozens of them himself. The path up to the crest is so heavily trafficked that it's like a regular road. You could lead a herd of cattle up to the summit.

"What was really incredible though was how easy it was to get down to the bottom of the pit—to the shore of the lake. Do you remember how hard it was the last time we were there?"

"You mean the level of the lake has risen that much?"

"No. It's still about 1,500 feet down, at least when we were there. And that wasn't very long ago. What has happened is that a large slab of rock has separated from the wall and broken into blocks separated by cracks. The whole thing forms a kind of staircase leading down to a pile of rubble and then to what we call the beach—a flat area about six feet above the lava lake. It's the easiest thing in the world to get down there by climbing from one block to another. The blocks are six feet apart at most, and go down in descending stages of about thirty feet. It looks hard, but it's not. They lead right down to the lake. But we had to stay a few feet away from the very edge of the lake because of the heat.

"The lake is now a huge crescent covering more than half of the pit's circumference. The other half is covered by a solid shell. There's a large round island in the middle, and its crest is as high as the terrace. You can reach its foot from the solid part of the lake. We tried to climb it, but we couldn't. It was like trying to climb a pile of red-hot plates."

If Laurent could not climb it, I knew then, it could not be climbed. In any case, it would have been nothing more than an interesting exercise in climbing. The island, I concluded, had been formed by a general rise in the magma chimney sometime between our 1972 expedition and the recent visit by Roland and Laurent. I learned later that there had, in fact, been such a rise in July, and that it had taken place under the startled gaze of a group of tourists standing on the crest.

"The lava overflowed twice onto the terrace," Laurent went on, "and left two very thin basalt crusts. There were several bubbles in the crusts, about six feet in diameter, and they were as fragile as glass. There had obviously been two wide streams, quite distinct from one another, and one of them reached a spot no more than twelve feet from the wall.''

When the magma retreated after that overflow, which seemed similar to the one we had seen in April 1972, the central part solidified and stayed at the level that it had reached. Then, as the level of the lake receded into the pit, this central mass protruded more and more until it resembled a steep tower. It was built up by the accumulation of thousands of streams from successive overflows—those fleeting inundations that we had witnessed in 1972. Unfortunately, no credible observer was present when the lake rose. It would seem that the liquid part of the chimney was ring-shaped, at least in its upper portion. The solid cylindrical ''stopper''—that is, Laurent's ''island''—probably, at a certain depth, rests on magma which, although it is no doubt molten, is of such high rigidity that it behaves like solid matter. Then, when the magma sinks sufficiently, the island sinks in turn into the cavity left by the magma. So far as the lake itself is concerned, we had already seen its annular form in June 1972, when the lava was hidden under a hard crust. Even before then, its morphology gave us clue to its shape. Ordinarily, only a variable part of the visible lake's surface consists of molten rock, and the rest is covered by a shell punctured by vents through which it is sometimes possible to see the flow of lava underneath. We had had that experience in 1959; now, fifteen years later, the lake was about 600 feet higher than it had been, and Laurent and Roland had seen the same thing.

Child's play

''Getting down to the lake was child's play,'' Laurent repeated happily. ''I can't get over it, when I think of the problems we had in 1972. We spent three days in the caldera and slept in a little tent that had been left on the terrace by some tourists. It was a shambles and had been eaten away by the sulfuric acid. Naturally, it was raining, and we were soaked, but we didn't care. It was great just being there. And there was no one else around! You can imagine what that was like, after the mob we had in 1972. No tourists at all. I don't think the ban on tourists will last though. The attendants in the park make too much money from tourists to keep them out for very long. They charge 10 zaires ($20) a head, and that doesn't include meals. The money, of course, goes straight into their pockets. I can't be-

lieve they're willing to give up that much money. I'm sure the day will come when Nyiragongo will be crawling with tourist safaris and self-styled volcanologists, just like Etna."

"What about the overflows?" I asked.

"There weren't any. At least, not in the three days we were there. And none when we went back, two weeks later, after a tour of Nyamuragira, Visoke, Karisimbi, and Mikeno. There had been variations in the lake's level, but none greater than those you saw in 1958 and 1959. The highest it rose was about five feet. Of course, even then we had to move back because of the heat. It was the same when lava began to shoot out of the geysers in the lake. We had to get out of there in a hurry. The globs of hot lava were flying over our heads only a few yards away. I've never seen lava so yellow. It looked like bright gold. How hot do you think it was? Probably over 1,100°C, don't you think? There was something strange about the lake. It looked like a rosary of bubbles, all flowing in the same direction. And at the tip they all clustered together. There was a very loud rumbling, like thunder."

We had often seen these "floating geysers." There are two possible explanations. They may be the result of a pocket of liquid lava in the process of losing its gas while surrounded by a mass of lava that is already degassed. Or, they may be caused by pieces of rock that the lava has torn from the walls. In that case, the rocks were losing their oxygen, which was causing the bubbles. Scoria often contains large quantities of bubbles filled with air. The fact that these floating geysers tend to cluster at the mouth of the tunnel into which the current flows would incline me to the second hypothesis. What bothers me, though, is the fact that we have never caught a glimpse even of the tip of one of these hypothetical submerged rocks. In "normal" volcanoes, such as Etna and Nyamuragira, and elsewhere, lava streams contain blocks of rock covered with fresh lava, moving along with the current. Most of these rocks are submerged, but you can see part of them protruding above the surface. At Nyiragongo, however, we had never seen any such rocks. So, I would accept the first hypothesis: that the geysers are caused by large pockets of lava rich in gas. This lava would tend to rise to the surface because it is less dense than the gas-free lava that forms the bulk of the lake. As it rises, the pressure on it decreases and it begins to effervesce, which would explain the bubbles. And, of course, the pockets of lava move with the current, unlike the stationary geysers located above dikes that open onto the floor of the lake. I do not claim that

A volcanologist's dream.

that is the true explanation for the floating geysers of Nyiragongo, but it is the only one that I can devise at this time.

Laurent brought me the last reliable news that I had of Nyiragongo. I cannot help but think of the rare and valuable opportunities for observation that we lose over the years. Nyiragongo's activity, characterized by variations in intensity but also by constant emanations of gas, could teach us so much. I still dream of a continuous study of the Virunga volcanoes, and especially of Nyiragongo; of building an effective observatory open to competent researchers from all countries. But I realize that, for the present, it is no more than a dream. It is not Nyiragongo itself that keeps the

Appendices
and
Glossary

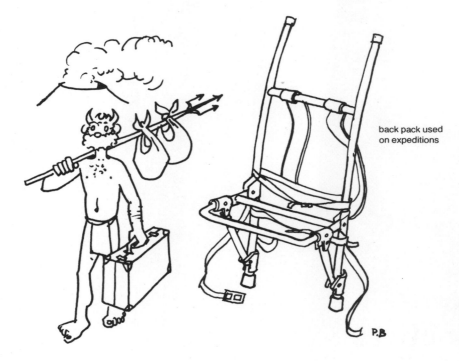

back pack used
on expeditions

P.B

Appendix I

THE TECHNIQUES OF THE VOLCANOLOGIST

What is the point of volcanological expeditions? The study of volcanoes helps us to understand volcanism, which is a major geological phenomenon. Volcanism, in fact, governs the expansion of the ocean floors, and thus is a factor in the movement of tectonic plates and the formation of ridges and trenches where mountain ranges are born. It has a hand in the genesis of metallic ores and in the composition of the earth's crust. It is at the basis of high-energy geothermic domes. It also represents a serious danger.

All of these factors justify our efforts to understand this essential phenomenon, and also warrant efforts incomparably greater than those now being made.

Our own work is aimed at discovering a few of the laws governing eruptions. For that purpose, we are trying to measure variations in they dynamic and energetic factors of volcanism; that is, the composition of the eruptive gases and the delivery of matter and energy in eruptions. We are attempting to gather that data where they are most meaningful, which is to say at the mouth of the eruptions themselves, since we do not have access to the deep source of the eruptions.

If we are to attain these goals, we must have the proper techniques both to approach these places and to gather valid data once we are there. Such techniques are being developed both in our laboratories and in the field. The first thing is to get to the place where we can get meaningful samplings—a place where access is difficult and more or less dangerous. For this, we use both mountain climbing and speleological techniques (climbing, ladders, winches, etc.). Then, once we reach the proper spot, we must take precautions against gases, volcanic ash, and heat. For the gases, we use either filtered gas masks (when the concentration of gases is not high) and automatic closed-circuit breathing apparatuses. To protect ourselves against lava splashes, hot ash, and similar volcanic by-products, we use full fiberglass helmets that are supported by the wearer's shoulders rather than by his head because the dorsal vertebrae have a higher tolerance for certain kinds of shock than the cervical vertebrae. The heat radiated by incandescent lava makes it necessary for us to wear heat-resistant suits. Until 1972, these suits were made of asbestos (a nonflammable mineral fiber) covered by a layer of aluminum, which served as a heat-reflector. The problem with these suits was that they were heavy and hot. Since 1972, we have used suits made of Nomex, which is a light, supple, and nonflammable synthetic material first developed for use by astronauts. The volcanologist's face is protected by a visor of glass plated with a thin (and therefore transparent) sheet of gold. Gold is an excellent deflector of heat. The heat of the ground in a volcano is not a serious problem so long as you don't stand still for too long a period. We wear ordinary mountain climbing shoes with Vibram soles, and these are adequate for a floor-temperature of 700°F to 800°F. Beyond those temperatures, we wear ice shoes, the ten tiny cleats of which form the only point of contact with the ground and conduct only a minimum of heat. With these, we can walk around for hours on rocks at 1,200°F to 1,800°F.

Taking measurements and readings, however, requires some sophisticated equipment. What we measure, essentially, is the temperature of the lava, and the temperature, flow, pressure, and chemical composition of gases. We make estimates—general estimates—of the speed and viscosity of lava. We take samplings of lava. We "listen" to the depths of the volcano by various geophysical methods: seismography, magnetometry, gravimetry, olinometry. And sometimes we undertake topographical surveys.

Temperatures can be taken either at a distance or else by means of a thermometer inserted directly into the lava or the gas. The pyroscope, which is used for long-distance measurement of an incandescent body (but not for gas), is used by most volcanologists because it makes it unnecessary for the researcher to expose himself to the discomforts and the dan-

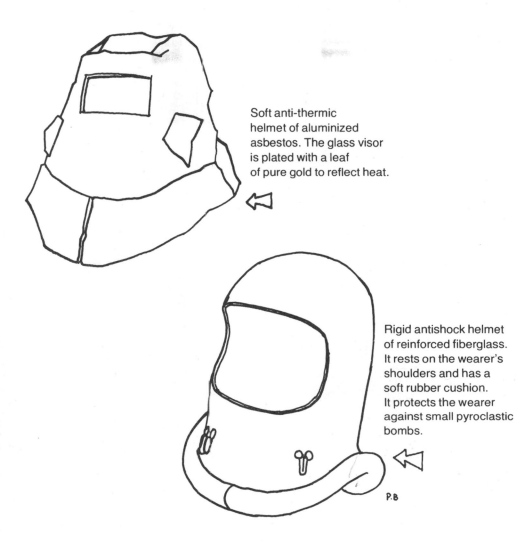

Soft anti-thermic
helmet of aluminized
asbestos. The glass visor
is plated with a leaf
of pure gold to reflect heat.

Rigid antishock helmet
of reinforced fiberglass.
It rests on the wearer's
shoulders and has a
soft rubber cushion.
It protects the wearer
against small pyroclastic
bombs.

P.B

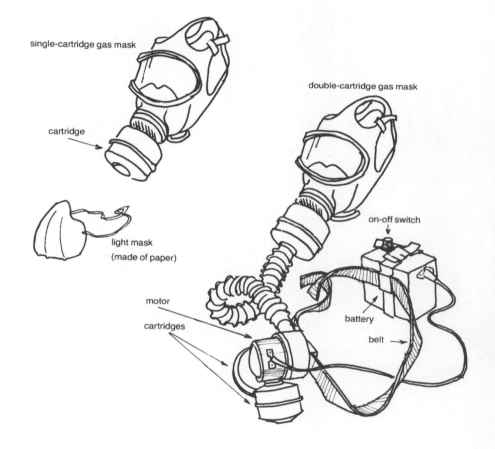

single-cartridge gas mask

cartridge

light mask
(made of paper)

double-cartridge gas mask

on-off switch

motor

cartridges

battery

belt

gers entailed in actually getting to the spot that is being studied. The pyroscope's readings, however, are very much influenced by the degree of transparency of the air between the eye of the observer and the point observed. Vapor and smoke are prejudicial to accurate readings. Also, the pyroscope's readings are based on a comparison between the lava and a wire brought to incandescence by means of an electric current—a subjective operation which sometimes results in major errors. We have therefore completely given up using the pyroscope and, to take readings at spots that we cannot reach ourselves, we use various kinds of infrared radiometers. There are some inconveniences also in using radiometers. They are heavy, cumbersome, fragile, and very expensive. They do, however, take accurate readings, and they produce accurate temperature charts, which is sometimes a very important consideration. When the point that we want to study is physically accessible to us, we use thermocouples, or pyrometric rods. These are special metal thermometers that give readings with a high level of precision. They also have the advantage of being able to take readings below the surface both in lava and in jets of gas, which means that, in addition to the temperature at the surface, we can take gradient readings.

The velocity of gas is an important factor because of the information it provides on both pressure and delivery. The velocity of gas is not easy to measure at a volcanic mouth, but we eventually developed two effective techniques for doing so. The first method involves the use of a very special kind of anemometer designed by Pierre Zettwoog, which measures variations in the speed of gases, but which can be used only when the gas jet itself is accessible. The second method is much more complex and requires a very elaborate optical and electronic hookup, which is another way of saying that it is very costly, fragile, and heavy. It does, however, make it possible to take long-distance readings. The apparatus in question is a telescope designed by Camille Vavasseur and Michael Beck of the University of Bradford. The telescope has the enormous advantage—a potential advantage, I should say, not yet realized at this time—of being able simultaneously to take temperature readings of the gases and to analyze and keep a running record of their chemical composition.

This instrument, unfortunately, was not yet operational when we were at Nyiragongo in 1972. We therefore had to study the chemical composition of gases by the classic method of taking samplings which were later subjected to laboratory analysis. These samplings were taken in special high-vacuum bottles. The techniques of sampling and analysis were progressively refined so as to avoid all kind of errors which, until then, affected the value of the results obtained.

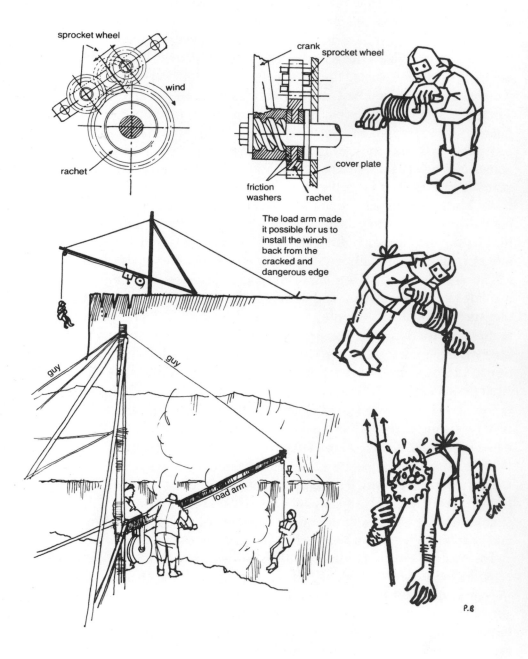

sprocket wheel

wind

rachet

crank sprocket wheel

cover plate

friction
washers rachet

The load arm made
it possible for us to
install the winch
back from the
cracked and
dangerous edge

guy

guy

load arm

P.B

Appendix II

DEPTH WINCHES

by Corentin Queffélec, engineer

A depth winch is an ensemble of two mechanically connected parts. The *hauler* is an assembly of trapezoidal rowels activated by a motor that transforms exponentially, as a function of the arc rolled, the effort expended ($T°$) on an object hauled (T). The *roller* exerts, behind the hauler, the effort $T°$ positive or negative in accordance with which the cable is raised or lowered and rolled up on a large drum spool along its entire length.

This principle, long known, makes possible the automatic and continuous rolling up of great lengths of cable, since, when it reaches the spool, the cable is no longer the seat of a very weak $T°$ effort and can thus roll up without difficulty in multiple layers.

The difficulty with winches lies not in the basic concept of the winch itself, but in the amount of stress to which the parts will be subjected—because the designer of a winch used to raise and lower weights in a crater, for example, usually does not know:

(a) The depth to which loads are to be lowered. It is true that this factor is known as soon as the first load is lowered, but until then, there is a margin of error which is often surprisingly large.

(b) The weight of the load to be hauled. For purposes of haulage, the actual weight is not only of the load itself, but the amount of added resistance resulting from, for example, the rubbing of the cable against a rocky wall, or the particular choice of route taken by a man being lowered into a crater. Such factors may vary so widely as to be beyond sound hypothetical calculation.

(c) The precise maneuver to be executed. Here, it is the load that dictates the maneuver, and the operator of the winch must simply follow its lead. Finally, it must be taken into account—and I know that operators of winches will bear me out on this—that raising or lowering a man on a cable involves "playing" the load, in somewhat the same way that a fisherman plays a game fish—only that, in the former case, the operator must sometimes work for hours without even *seeing* the load.

The kind of winch that we are talking about is not in general use, although it has had some industrial application especially in hauling because of a rather peculiar property: when $T°$ or T is nullified, T or $T°$ is also nullified, since the $\frac{T}{T°}$ relationship remains constant. This means that if you stop feeding out cable, the winch will stop delivering cable, with the result that there is no tangling or knotting or breaking of the cable. By the same token, if the hauler-drum assembly breaks down, the winch stops feeding cable and thus avoids twisting, knotting, etc., inside the winch.

Options

Obviously, a winch can have a manually operated drum or an automatic drum, independently of whether the winch itself is operated manually or electrically.

In the manual version, the drum is worked by hand separately from the hauler. The operation therefore requires three men: two working the cranks, which develop the hauling effort, and one at the drum which provides the cable's $T°$ effort.

In the automatic version, the $T°$ effort is provided automatically for both raising and lowering by two automatically selected connections. As a general rule, when the winch is operated manually, so is the drum; and the motor-operated winch is completely automatic.

The safety brake

With an arm-winch, it is simply not safe to rely on the usual band brake or catch to hold a load and keep it steady.

I place my own trust in the old-fashioned automatic brake used in almost all the cogwheel arm hoists such as those manufactured by Etablissements Verlinde, a well-known French company. So long as the proper adjustments are made, operation is quite reliable. To raise a load, the crank turns on the pinion gear and exerts pressure on the rachet. The three gears then disengage, and rotation is possible. To lower a load, the three gears engage and keep the rachet from turning. The crank loosens, releasing the rachet and making it possible for the pinion gear to turn and feed out cable. Because of the weight of the load, there is a tendency for the cable to feed out faster than the crank is turned. When that happens, the pinion gear tightens on the crank and blocks the rachet, stopping the cable.

The volcano winch

When Haroun Tazieff asked me to design an apparatus capable of lowering people 650 feet over a lake of molten lava, all I actually had to do was select a solution from a spectrum of possibilities. The winch had to be portable, in disassembled pieces weighing no more than 30 to 40 kilograms (65 to 85 pounds) each. The only solution, therefore, was an arm winch with a manually operated drum.

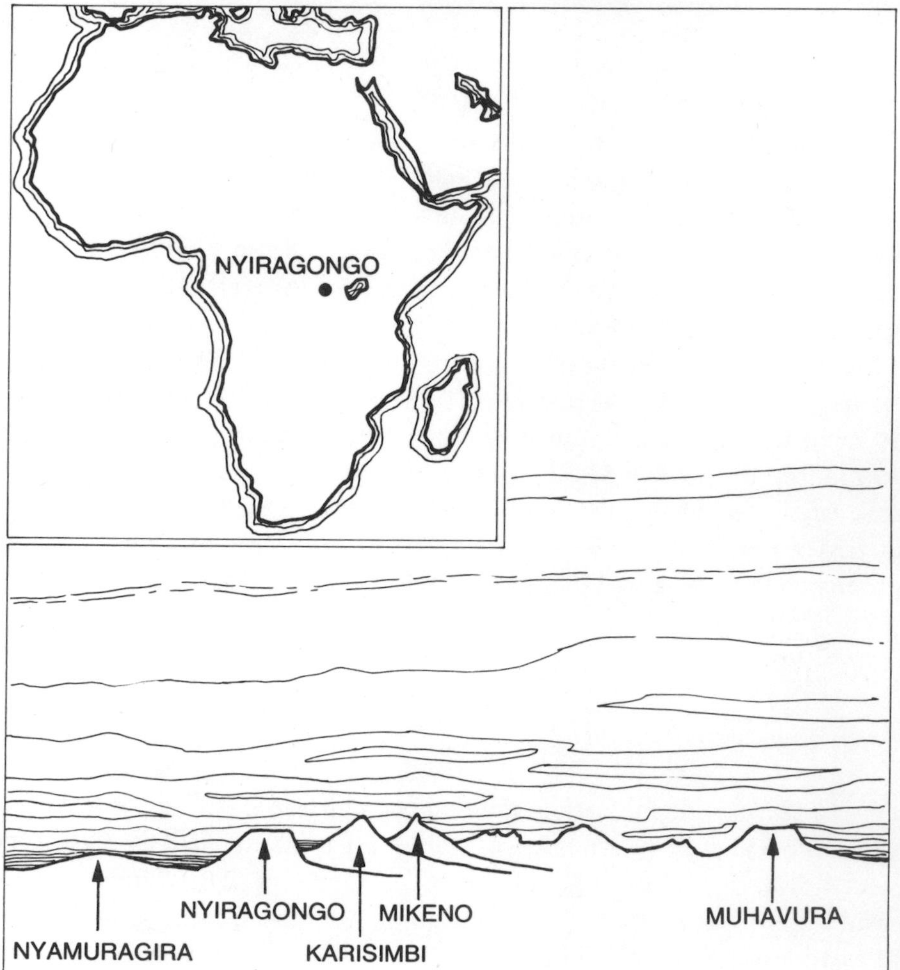

NYIRAGONGO

NYAMURAGIRA

NYIRAGONGO   MIKENO

KARISIMBI   MUHAVURA

THE VIRUNGA MOUNTAINS

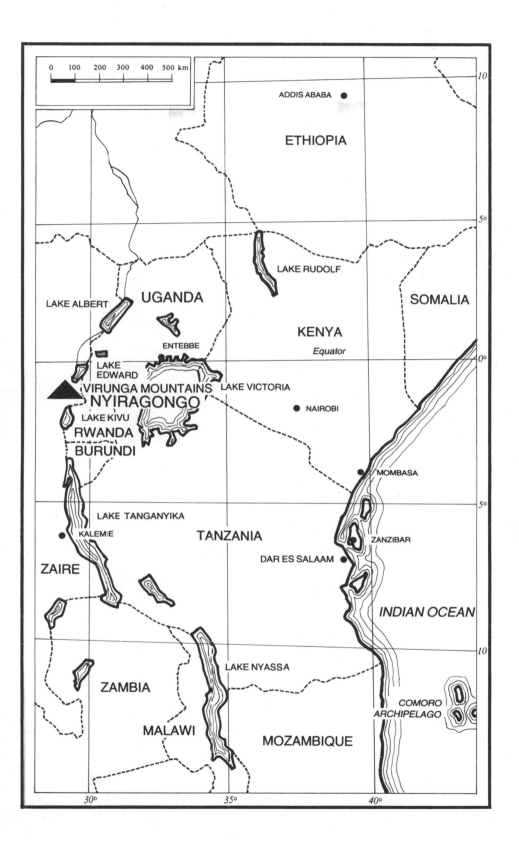

| 0 | 100 | 200 | 300 | 400 | 500 km |

ADDIS ABABA ●

ETHIOPIA

10

LAKE RUDOLF

5°

LAKE ALBERT

UGANDA

SOMALIA

KENYA

ENTEBBE

Equator

LAKE EDWARD

LAKE VICTORIA

0°

VIRUNGA MOUNTAINS
NYIRAGONGO

LAKE KIVU

NAIROBI ●

RWANDA
BURUNDI

MOMBASA ●

5°

LAKE TANGANYIKA

ZANZIBAR

KALEMIE ●

TANZANIA

DAR ES SALAAM ●

ZAIRE

INDIAN OCEAN

10

LAKE NYASSA

ZAMBIA

COMORO
ARCHIPELAGO

MALAWI

MOZAMBIQUE

30°

35°

40°

Appendix III

NYIRAGONGO

General observations

(a) *Location*. Nyiragongo is 11,380 feet above sea level and is located at 1°29′S and 29°14′E, in the central part of the Western Rift Valley of East Africa. This branch, which diverges from the Gregory Rift near the 5th parallel North and extends southward for over 900 miles, is the site of seismic activity that is exceptional in this otherwise very settled geological area. This activity is evidenced by the violent tremors (magnitude 7 and 7.2) of March 20 and May 17, 1966, which were probably caused by faults in the Ruwenzori Mountains.

Ninety miles to the south of these mountains, the ditch is intersected, from east to west, by a chain of eight powerful volcanoes known as the Virunga Mountains. With the possible exception of Mikeno (14,850 feet), which has been deeply cut by erosion, these volcanoes are regarded as active. However, except for a brief eruption of Mugogo (August 1, 1957), six miles from the summit of Visoke, only the two easternmost volcanoes, Nyamuragira (9,900 feet) and Nyiragongo (11,380 feet) have manifested any intense activity during the relatively brief historical period of this area. Between 1890 and 1974, there were a dozen eruptions and some intermittent activity of the lava lake.

The Virunga volcanoes probably go back no further than the Pliocene epoch. They were built up by lava flows that crossed and covered preexisting formations, some of them very ancient (Precambrian) and the others of more recent origin (fillings of the rift from the Tertiary and Quaternary periods).

The rocks produced by the collapse of the rift belong to the Ruzizian system (quartzites, metamorphic schists, and gneiss) and to the Urundian or Karagwe-Ankole systems (schists, quartzites, and dolomite limestone).

The rocks of the Ruzizian system are mixed with old granites the pebbles of which are found in the basic conglomerate of the Urundian system. The latter, in turn, is mixed with more recent granites. Finally, intrusions of carbonatite, of unknown age, crop up to the north of the chain, in the eastern end of the rift valley.

The rift itself contains a relatively thick sedimentary deposit, composed of Pleistocene gravel, sand, and clay.

The great mass of the Virunga Mountains rose on that base, or on one or the other part of it. The very special nature of the volcanoes' lavas is perhaps connected with that underlayer. As far as Nyiragongo itself is concerned, analysis of the allogenic enclaves of *pyroclastic* bombs thrown off by the caldera and by its satellite Ndosho, situated almost nine miles to the south-southwest, demonstrates that the conduit through which the cones are fed very likely crosses granitoid rocks similar to those which lie at the surface a few miles to the southeast (hologeucocrate granites, granites or gneiss rich in biotite, perhaps sillimanite gneiss, cordierite and spinel, or even pegmatites and filonian quartz). Nyiragongo's very active neighbor, Nyamuragira, on the other hand, probably rests on schists and quartzites of the Urundian group, which form the eastern face of the rift.

(b) *Description*. The Nyiragongo mountain comprises three truncated main cones, almost in a straight six-mile line running from south to north (actually, slightly northeast) and mostly parallel to the principal extension of the rift. It also has close to a hundred satellite cones of much smaller size, divided into two areas by deep fissure zones, running approximately north-south and southwest-northeast, and covering an area of about 200 square miles.

The principal cone is Nyiragongo itself. On either side of Nyiragongo are the two satellite cones, Shaheru to the south (9,240 feet) and Baruta to the north (10,230 feet). Both these two dormant volcanoes have huge craters that are now filled with vegetation. Shaheru's crater is 2,310 feet wide and averages approximately 265 feet in depth except at the saddle which connects it to Nyiragongo's slopes, where its wall is buried in lava from Nyiragongo. Baruta's crater is 3,630 feet in diameter and 1,000 feet deep. Its northwest wall is fissured and cut by dikes. The wall lies in the extension of the large fissure area which affects neighboring Nyamuragira.

The slopes of Nyiragongo are at an angle of 10° to 15° in their lower section, and rise progressively to an angle of 30° to 32°—and as high as 40° on the south-southwest side. The base of the peak blends imperceptibly into the surrounding plain which was formed from innumerable lava flows, intersecting and overlapping from Nyiragongo's three major cones and its smaller satellites, as well as from the larger neighboring volcanoes and their own satellites: Nyamuragira to the northwest, Karisimbi (14,850 feet) to the east, and Mikeno (14,700 feet) to the east-northeast.

Nyiragongo itself is a strato volcano topped by a caldera 4,125 feet in diameter and 3,630 feet deep. Its interior wall, with an average height of 560 feet, ends at a horizontal terrace approximately 660 feet wide. A crevasse separates the terrace from the wall of the caldera, similar to that found in glaciers and is a result of the weakening and partial collapse of the rock strata. The terrace circumscribes a round pit with vertical walls some 2,250 feet across and 600 feet deep. The floor of the pit is covered partly by a lake of molten lava and partly by a block of solidified lava, broken into sections, which forms a floating island in the lake. The caldera and the pit are the result of the sinking *en masse* of the upper part of the volcano, probably following the withdrawal of the magma chimney. The horizontal terraces are the remnants of earlier lava lakes. The island floats in the molten lava because the rocks that make up the island apparently have a lower density (because of their vesicularity) than that of the molten lava.

Activity

(a) *History.* In 1894, when it was discovered by von Götzen, Nyiragongo had two adjacent central craters, separated only by a thin partition. One of these craters emitted vapor. Since that time, reports of observers have been sporadic and of very variable reliability. The following is a synopsis of the volcano's history based on those reports:

1904-1907: dormant.

1908-1915: vapor.

1918: the two craters were united when the partition that had separated them collapsed.

1916-1924: smoke.

1924-1928: dormant.

1928: from this time probably dates the existence of the lake of lava. This deduction is based on the fact that the volcano was now smoking permanently and that the smoke had a reddish glow.

1948 (July): the lake of lava, viewed for the first time, was 600 feet below the level of the upper terrace, and the molten lava lapped at the base of the wall. The surface of the lake covered approximately 396,000 square feet (Tazieff, 1949).

1953 (August): the lake had shrunk to about 198,000 square feet, and was about sixty feet lower, thereby exposing a second terrace (Tazieff, unpublished).

1956 (February): the lake was at more than 132 feet below the second terrace (Sahama and Meyer, 1958).

1956 (July): the lake was more than 100 feet below the second terrace. (This statement is, in my opinion, subject to doubt.)

1958 (July, August): the lake was about 100 feet lower than the second terrace and there were two islands near the southern end of the lake. The surface of the lake was approximately 62,700 square feet (de Magnée, 1959).

1959 (July, August): the lake has shrunk to 42,900 square feet, exposing a third terrace. The islands have been transformed into peninsulas, and the lake is now 132 feet below the second terrace (Wiser, 1962). The level of the lake varies upward or downward, in a very short interval, by nine feet, over a six-week period during which it was under practically continuous observation.

1965 (March): the lake has risen to about thirty-five feet below the second terrace.

1965 (December): the lake has risen level with the second terrace.

1966 (February): the lake has risen to a level thirty-five to sixty feet above the second terrace. Its surface, covered by a thin shell of solidified lava, is 565 square feet. Powerful gas activity concentrated in a dozen vents, with certain vents giving off a continuous stream of lava drops, ashes, and flames (Bonnet, 1966, and Tazieff, unpublished).

1966 (August): activity very similar to that of February, but there are fewer vents and the flow of gas is apparently more concentrated (Bonnet, 1966).

1971 (January): the lake is about fifty feet below the first terrace (600 feet below the rim of the caldera).

1972 (April): the first terrace is covered by the lake, the level of which is 600 feet below the rim.

1972 (June): the lake is 100 feet below the second terrace (710 feet below the rim of the caldera).

1972 (August): the lake is 165 feet below the second terrace (742 feet below the rim).

1974 (July): the lake is level with the second terrace (610 feet below the rim).

1974 (September): the lake is about 130 feet below the second terrace (740 feet below the rim), and the summit of the island is level with the second terrace.

(b) *The floating island.* This island, as we have pointed out, probably is a collapsed vestige of the central part of the upper terrace. It not only rises and sinks with the level of the lake, but sometimes also has other kinds of movement. It rotates, as evidenced by surveys (Wiser, 1961; Thonnard, 1965), up to 11° in 347 days (for an average of two feet per day). It also moves horizontally. In 1948, its eastern tip was touching the second wall, and by 1953, it had floated about 100 feet westward, thus allowing the formation of a second terrace. Between 1958 and August 1959, it moved another few yards toward the west, during the formation of the third terrace.

The circumference of the island is marked by a half-dozen vents giving off gas under pressure at temperatures in the neighborhood of 1,000°C. It appears, though this has not yet been proved, that currents of molten lava move around the island beneath the surface. The island was entirely covered by lava flows in 1971. A new island was formed in 1972, by the build-up of large streams of lava from overflows. In September 1974, it was tower-shaped and about 130 feet in height.

(c) *Movements and temperatures of the lake.* Since 1948, the year of its discovery, the lake has been the site of more or less intense activity. This activity is characterized by alternating periods of calm and agitation.

The changes in the lake's level have been of major proportions. Sometimes these changes have been on the order of 200 feet over a period of weeks or months, and sometimes of three to 20 feet over a period of one hour or less. It happens sometimes that the lava "rises," like dough, for several inches or a foot, while it is being observed.

Some authors use the word *cycle* to describe such behavioral alternates.

In this case, that term should not be taken to indicate regularity of recurrence. The cycle we are talking about generally has the characteristics described below, which are quite similar to those observed at the lava lake of Kilauea, except that at Nyiragongo, the lava has never been observed to pour into the lake from a vent located in the wall.

During periods of calm, the surface of the lake is covered by a plastic crust of rock, usually broken by narrow cracks spreading over a radius of several hundred feet. It happens rarely that, at the end of a sufficiently long period of calm, the crust solidifies into a shell of dermolithic lava. The temperature of the crust varies in accordance with several factors, the most important of which is the thickness of the crust itself. Guy Bonnet (1960), using a thermo-electric receiver to measure the overall radiation, obtained a minimum reading of 956°K (683°C or 1,261°F) for an opaque section of shell, and a maximum of 1,134°K (861°C +/ − 40°; or 1,582°F +/ − 104°) for a semiopaque section. These readings were taken at subvertical distances of 250 to 400 feet. A. Delsemme (1960), using an optic pyrometer, found an average temperature of 820°K (547°C or 1,017°F), while, by means of direct thermocouple readings, he registered a temperature of 650°C (1,202°F) for a skin formed one hour earlier; 840°C (1,544°F) for a thinner skin of undetermined age; and 980°C (1,796°F) for a skin covering lava in movement.

The sampling rod makes it possible to take gas samplings from vents in perfect safety.

The gases are put into the bottle by perforating the rubber stopper with a hollow needle which is worked mechanically.

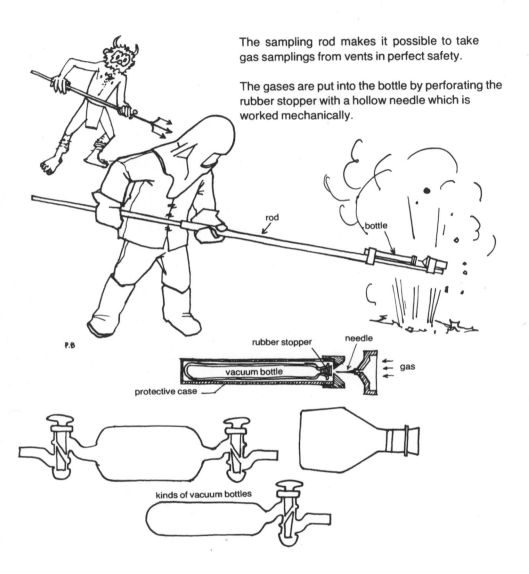

rod

bottle

rubber stopper

needle

vacuum bottle

gas

protective case

P.B

kinds of vacuum bottles

The seismograph is used to measure the intensity of the shock waves that characterize an earthquake. The readings of several seismographs make it possible to determine the epicenter of the earthquake.

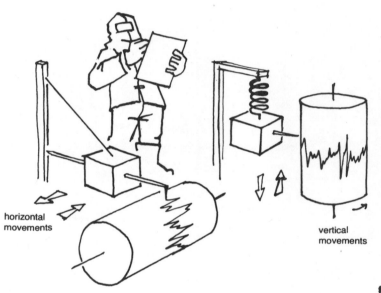

horizontal
movements

vertical
movements

P. B.

Gravimetry measures variations in the intensity of weight at different points of the earth's surface.

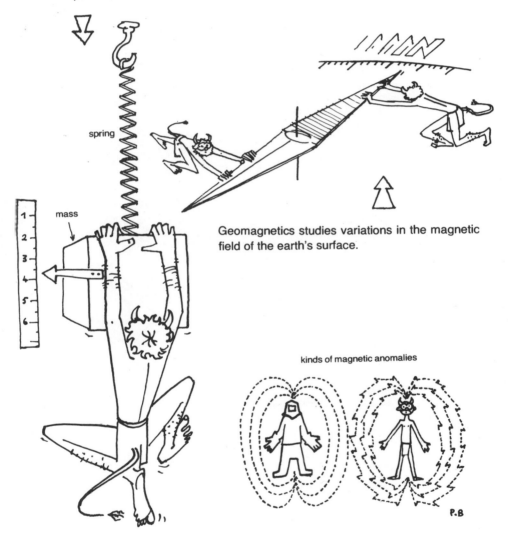

spring

mass

Geomagnetics studies variations in the magnetic field of the earth's surface.

kinds of magnetic anomalies

P.B

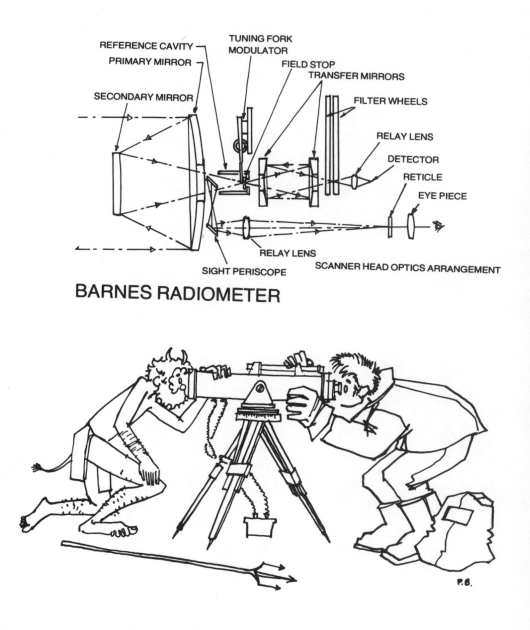

BARNES RADIOMETER

GEOCHEMISTRY!

Glossary

ANEMOMETER
An instrument used to measure the speed of escaping gas and, more particularly, the velocity of the wind.

ASH, VOLCANIC
A particle of lava, less than 4mm in diameter, that has been shot up into the air and has fallen back down.

BASALT
A rock formed from magma, composed primarily of calcic plagioclase and pyroxene. A dark, fine-grained rock.

BIOTITE
A mineral of the mica group, containing potassium phyllosilicate, aluminum, magnesium, and iron.

BOLOMETER
An electric thermometer for measuring infrared radiation.

CALDERA
A caldera is a very large, basin-shaped volcanic crater. One way that a caldera is formed is when the sides of a crater collapse, thus forming the larger opening.

MAGNETIC ANOMALY
Evidence of a departure from the normal magnetism of the earth.

MAGNETOMETER
An insturment for measuring the components of the earth's magnetic field.

MANTLE
The part of the earth's interior situated between the crust and the core. The core begins at a depth of almost 2,000 miles.

NEPHELINE
A mineral consisting of silicate of sodium but poor in silica.

OBSIDIAN
Volcanic glass, which is formed from lava that cooled very rapidly.

OPTIC PYROMETER
Instrument for long-distance measuring of the temperature of incandescent objects. The color of the object is compared to that of an electric wire raised to incandescence by means of a current of known intensity.

PEGMATITE
A coarse-grained rock characterized by large crystals. The large crystals were formed under the earth's surface.

PLATE TECTONICS
The theory that the earth's crust is made up of separate plates that abut and move in relation to one another.

PYROCLASTIC BOMBS
Fragments of lava ejected from a volcano during an eruption.

PYROMETER
An instrument for measuring high temperatures.

PYROSCOPE
An optic pyrometer.

QUARTZITE
A rock composed of grains of sand cemented by silica.

RADIOMETER
An instrument for measuring radiated energy.

RIFT
A large ditch formed by the sinking of a portion of the earth's crust or the separation of the earth's plates.

SADDLE
A ridge connecting two higher elevations.

SEISMOGRAPH
An instrument used to record waves produced by seismic shocks.

SILL
A horizontal intrusion of igneous rock between strata of older rock.

SILLIMANITE
A mineral containing aluminum silicate.

SPINEL
A mineral consisting essentially of aluminum and magnesium.

STRATO VOLCANO
A volcano formed by alternating strata of lava and strata of volcanic ash.

STRATUM
A layer of rock. (pl. strata)

THEODOLITE
A geodesic instrument used for measuring angles.

THERMOCOUPLE
An instrument made of two different metals welded together which, by transforming heat into electric current, makes it possible to measure very high temperatures (also called a thermoelectric couple).

TRACHYTE
A volcanic rock rich in feldspar and devoid of quartz.

TUFF
A rock formed from finer kinds of pyroclastic materials, primarily ash and lapilli.

VENT
A mouth or opening exhaling gases or spewing lava (also called a *blowhole*).

VESICULARITY
The quality of containing vesicles or air cavities.

VISCOSITY
The resistance of a fluid to flow.

Bibliography

HOLMES, A. and HARWOOD, H.F. *The Volcanic Area of Bufumbira.* Geological Survey of Uganda. III (1936).

SAHAMA, Th. G. *Petrology of Mt. Nyiragongo: A Review.*

Edinburgh Geological Society 19:1 (1962).

———, and MEYER, A. *Study of the Volcano Nyiragongo: A Progress Report.* Belgian Congo: Institute des Parcs Nationale, 1958.

Photographic Credits

page 8: M. Vaucher; page 12: H. Tazieff; page 16: H. Tazieff; page 18: H. Tazieff, H. Tazieff; page 19: A. de Munck; page 22: H. Tazieff; page 23: H. Tazieff; page 25: H. Tazieff; page 26: H. Tazieff; page 27: H. Tazieff; page 31: A. de Munck; page 34: H. Tazieff; page 39: H. Tazieff; page 41: H. Tazieff; page 42: H. Tazieff; page 44: H. Tazieff; page 46: H. Tazieff; page 47: H. Tazieff; page 49: H. Tazieff, H. Tazieff; page 51: H. Tazieff, H. Tazieff; page 52: H. Tazieff; page 53: H. Tazieff; page 54: H. Tazieff; page 56: H. Tazieff; page 57: H. Tazieff; page 61: H. Tazieff, H. Tazieff; page 64: H. Tazieff, H. Tazieff; page 66: H. Tazieff, H. Tazieff; page 67: H. Tazieff: page 70: H. Tazieff; page 71: H. Tazieff, H. Tazieff; page 74: H. Tazieff; page 75: H. Tazieff; page 78: H. Tazieff; page 79: C. Tulpin; page 81: H. Tazieff; page 84: C. Tulpin; page 86: H. Tazieff; page 89: H. Tazieff, H. Tazieff; page 91: H. Tazieff, H. Tazieff, H. Tazieff; page 92: H. Tazieff; page 93: H. Tazieff; page 95: H. Tazieff; page 96: C. Tulpin, H. Tazieff; page 97: H. Tazieff, H. Tazieff; page 100: H. Tazieff; page 101: H. Tazieff; page 104: H. Tazieff; page 105: H. Tazieff; page 108: H. Tazieff; page 109: H. Tazieff, H. Tazieff; page 112: H. Tazieff, H. Tazieff; page 114: A. Delsemme; page 115: H. Tazieff; page 116: H. Tazieff; page 117: H. Tazieff; page 118: H. Tazieff; page 121: H. Tazieff; page 122: H. Tazieff, H. Tazieff; page 123: H. Tazieff, H. Tazieff; page 124: H. Tazieff; page 126: H. Tazieff; page 127: H. Tazieff; page 129: H. Tazieff; page 132: H. Tazieff, H. Tazieff; page 133: H. Tazieff, H. Tazieff; page 136: H. Tazieff; page 139: H. Tazieff; page 140: H. Tazieff, H. Tazieff; page 141: H. Tazieff; page 144: H. Tazieff; page 151: H. Tazieff; page 152: C. Tulpin; page 154: H. Tazieff; page 155: H. Tazieff; page 157: H. Tazieff; page 158: H. Tazieff, L. Bichet; page 159: H. Tazieff; page 161: L. Bichet; page 164: E.E.I.; page 165: L. Bichet; page 168: D. Cavillon; page 172: R. Citron; page 175: H. Tazieff; page 176: A. de Munck; page 177: L. Bichet, H. Tazieff; page 178: D. Cavillon, H. Tazieff; page 179: L. Bichet, H. Tazieff, Fanfan; page 180: M. Loye; page 181: M. Vaucher, Ch. Vioujard; page 184: L. Bichet; page 185: M. Loye; page 188: M. Loye; page 192: Fanfan; page 196: M. Vaucher, M. Loye; page 197: M. Loye; page 200: D. Cavillon, Ch. Vioujard-Gamma; page 201: L. Bichet; page 203: Fanfan, Fanfan; page 204: D. Cavillon; page 205: Fanfan; page 207: M. Loye; page 208: Fanfan; page 209: Fanfan, Ch. Vioujard-Gamma; page 211: M. Loye; page 213: Fanfan, H. Tazieff; page 214: M. Loye; page 215: L. Bichet; page 218: D. Cavillon; page 222: M. Loye; page 223: L. Bichet; page 226: M. Loye; page 230: M. Loye; page 231: H. Tazieff; page 232: D. Cavillon; page 233: M. Loye; page 234: D. Cavillon, M. Vaucher; page 235: D. Cavillon; page 238: Ch. Vioujard; page 239: M. Vaucher; page 240: H. Tazieff; page 242: H. Tazieff; page 244: A. de Munck, A. de Munck; page 245: A. de Munck; page 248: D. Cavillon; page 250: A. de Munck; page 252: W. Bonatti; page 254: A. de Munck; page 256: H. Tazieff.

Jacket photo by M. Loye
Inside flap photo by Ch. Vioujard-Gamma

Dépôt légal 2e trimestre 1975 – Flammarion, éditeur, N° 10203 – N° d'imp. : 7203
Imprimerie Déchaux, Aulnay-sous-Bois